PACCA SERIES ON THE DOMESTIC ROOTS
OF UNITED STATES FOREIGN POLICY

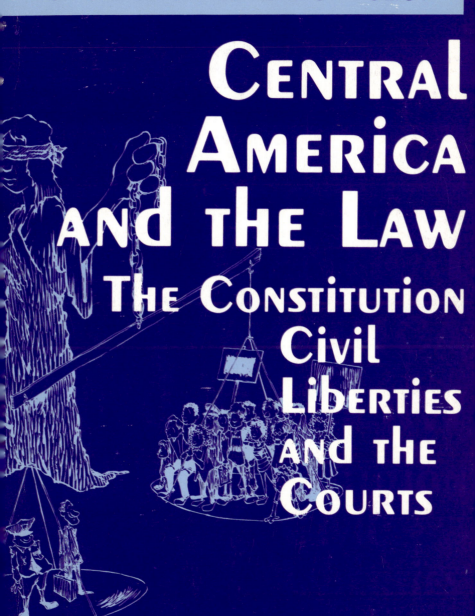

CENTRAL AMERICA and the LAW

The Constitution Civil Liberties and the Courts

MARK TUSHNET

PACCA SERIES ON THE DOMESTIC ROOTS OF U.S. FOREIGN POLICY

Central America and the Law

The Constitution, Civil Liberties, and the Courts

Mark Tushnet

South End Press   **Boston, MA**

Cover graphic by John Klostner
Cover design by Greg Bates and Todd Jailer
Manufactured in the USA

Library of Congress Cataloging-in-Publication Data
Tushnet, Mark V., 1945-
Central America and the law.
(PACCA series on the domestic roots of U.S. foreign policy)
Bibliography: p.
    1. United States--Foreign relations--Law and legislation. 2. Government, Resistance to--United States. 3. United States--Foreign relations--Nicaragua. 4. Nicaragua--Foreign relations--United States. I. Title. II. Series.
    KF4651.T87 1988   342.73'0412   88-6693
    ISBN 0-89608-340-3 (pbk.)   347.302412

South End Press, 116 Saint Botolph St., Boston, MA 02115

Policy Alternatives for the Caribbean and Central America:
  (PACCA)
  Suite 2
  1506 19th Street, NW
  Washington, D.C. 20036
  (202) 332-6333

Domestic Roots Statement

Domestic Roots of U.S. Foreign Policy is a project of Policy Alternatives for the Caribbean and Central America (PACCA), an association of scholars and policymakers. Through research, analysis, policy recommendations, and the collaboration of analysts in the U.S. and the Caribbean Basin, PACCA aims to promote a humane and democratic alternative to present U.S. policies toward Central America and the Caribbean.

The principles of such an alternative are set forth in PACCA's *Changing Course: Blueprint for Peace in Central America and the Caribbean*:

> U.S. foreign policy should be based on the principles which it seeks to further in the world. These include: non-intervention, respect for self-determination, collective self-defense, peaceful settlement of disputes, respect for human rights, support for democratic development and concern for democratic values. Adherence to these principles is critical to working out practical programs for regional peace and development.

Participants in the *Domestic Roots* project endorse these principles and seek to widen discussion of alternative policies based on them. The project explores the links between current U.S. policies in the region and major institutions and issues in U.S. domestic politics. In a series of pamphlets, *Domestic Roots* will highlight the continuity between domestic policy initiatives and current policies in the region, locate the domestic sources of current policy choices there, assess the obstacles to and opportunities for widening debate about those policies, and construct a decent and democratic alternative to them.

Acknowledgements

For their comments on drafts of this pamphlet, I would like to thank Judy Appelbaum, Bob Armstrong, Angie Berryman, Bob Borosage, Josh Cohen, Bill Davis, Cynthia Peters, Frances Fox Piven, Michael Ratner, Joel Rogers, Juliet Schor, and Bob Stark.

Table of Contents

INTRODUCTION

The Iran-contra hearings in 1987 were pervaded by discussions of law. In the course of examining the sale of United States weapons to Iran and the transfer of profits from that venture to support the contras in Nicaragua, the congressional committees examined the role of Lieutenant Colonel Oliver North, a central figure in these activities. Colonel North was on the staff of the President's National Security Council. The examination of Colonel North's activities rapidly descended into the details of various complex statutes, and the assessment of the legality of his activities came to turn on a minute inquiry into exactly what Congress had said and meant. In the Boland Amendment, Congress had prohibited United States support for the contras. Did Colonel North violate the Boland Amendment? Or was the Boland Amendment not applicable to the National Security Council? Or was it unconstitutional?

Questions about the meaning of the law arise outside the confines of the national policymaking process centered in Washington. For example, earlier in the year opponents of the activities of the Central Intelligence Agency, including Amy Carter and Abbie Hoffman, had been tried in Northampton, Massachusetts for their attempts to obstruct recruiting by the CIA. The judge allowed them to present evidence that what they had done was necessary to avoid the greater evil embodied in the CIA's activities, and a jury selected from a community that had undergone extensive political education and organization around the issue of the CIA acquitted the protestors even though obstruction had clearly occurred. (See Box One.)

These examples illustrate one of the central features of politics in the United States: Conflicts about policy often are presented as conflicts about what the law is or should be. That's because many people see law as a major means of controlling the exercise of arbitrary power. But they are often frustrated when they turn to the law because of the

1

Box One

The Northampton Trial

In the fall of 1986, demonstrators at the University of Massachusetts, who included Amy Carter and Abbie Hoffman, sat in at a University building to protest CIA recruiting on the campus. They were arrested for trespassing and disorderly conduct. At their trial in April 1987, the demonstrators acknowledged that they had indeed trespassed, but raised the defense of "necessity." That is, they claimed that their "illegal" act was justified because it was necessary in order to avert a more serious evil—the recruiting of employees who would engage in illegal activities by the CIA. The trial judge allowed the demonstrators to present their necessity defense, and they had various experts on CIA activities testify before the jury about illegal actions by the CIA. The jury, drawn from the residents of a campus-oriented community in Western Massachusetts, acquitted the demonstrators.

It's important to understand how this legal victory came about. The first thing to note is that the judge's willingness to allow the demonstrators to present the necessity defense is quite unusual. The defense was developed to handle cases like ones where mountain climbers stranded during a storm break into a cabin and eat the food they find there. They have committed crimes—trespass and theft—but they did so to avoid the greater evil of their impending death. With that sort of case in mind, it's clear why some rather stringent requirements are usually placed on the defense; typically the defendants are allowed to raise the defense only if they had no legal alternatives to breaking the law, only if the greater evil they were trying to avert was imminent, and only if there is a close connection between their illegal actions and the greater illegality they were trying to avert.

The Northampton case did not really satisfy any of these requirements. (And it might be contrasted with a fairly common situation these days, in which people charged with harrassing abortion clinics try to raise the defense of necessity—they say they are trying to avoid the greater harm of killing fetuses—but are not allowed by judges to present the defense.) So why was the defense allowed to be presented in the Northampton case? Basically, because the judge decided to allow it. If he had not, and the demonstrators had been convicted, there was almost no chance that they would have succeeded in persuading a higher court that the judge made a mistake in barring them from using the necessity defense. But then, why did the judge decide to allow them to use the defense? Because the local community was sympathetic to the defendants, and the judge knew it. (For additional discussion of the role of how local political circumstances affect decisions like this one, see Box Four.)

difficulty they have in persuading courts—and sometimes in persuading other people who might participate in a movement to oppose illegal activities by the United States government—that the activities are really illegal. (The Northampton example may not accurately describe the overall role that the law plays in the activities of the Central America Movement. When we return to the example in Chapter Four, however, we will see the trial's more general significance.)

The frustration of expectations about the law comes through in many Central America Movement (CAM) discussions about some central legal issues that have concerned it. People associated with the CAM often assert that the activities of the United States government in Central America are illegal, and yet they have been unable to make substantial headway with those assertions in the courts of the United States. It is not immediately apparent why this is so, for these assertions are supported by powerful legal arguments based on United States and international law.

- The International Court of Justice (the World Court) ruled that United States aid to the contras, and its support of attacks on Nicaraguan oil installations and ports, violated customary international law and the "general principles of humanitarian law."[1]

- The Boland Amendment prohibited the use of federal funds to support, "directly or indirectly, military or paramilitary operations in Nicaragua" during 1985 and 1986.[2] Oliver North directed to the contras some of the profits from the sale of arms to Iran, and helped construct and operate facilities to supply arms to the contras.[3]

- The Neutrality Act, in effect since 1794, makes it a crime for anyone in the United States to "prepare a means for or furnish money for" military expeditions against any foreign country "with whom the United States is at peace."[4] Numerous private organizations have raised money to purchase military supplies for the contras. Their efforts have been coordinated, to some extent, by government officials such as Colonel North.[5]

When we examine these claims more closely, some problems crop up. Most people, when hearing assertions about illegality, probably assume that courts will do something about the illegal activities. And they may assume that the legal assertions are so well supported that no one could reasonably disagree with the claims. But

- The United States government refused to comply with the World Court judgment, and a lawsuit in federal court to enforce the judgment has been dismissed.[6]

- Colonel North argued that he had not violated the Boland Amendment. (See Box Two.)

- The federal government has shown no inclination whatever to prosecute violations of the Neutrality Act, and the courts have held that they cannot order the government even to investigate well-founded allegations of such violations.[7]

- Lawyers for the CAM can develop legal theories that explain why courts ought to act against the actions of the executive branch, yet government lawyers can counter with their own theories that explain why no illegality has even occurred. (For example, government lawyers have argued that, for quite technical reasons, the World Court had no authority to issue its decision.[8] And they have insisted that World Court judgments are only advisory.)

Given all this, what exactly does it mean for the CAM to say that United States activities are illegal, and, more broadly, how should participants in the CAM think about the place that law has in movement work? In line with the aims of the Domestic Roots project, this pamphlet steps back from the details of the legal arguments to examine how and why it matters for the CAM to talk about law.[9]

The pamphlet's four chapters describe the structure of the legal system, the details of some areas of law particularly relevant to the CAM, and the opportunities for and limits upon the use of legal strategies to challenge United States foreign policy. The first chapter describes the constitutional system and the reasons why it is hard for the CAM to get the courts even to consider its legal arguments. The official rhetoric that the government adheres to the law contrasts dramatically with the persistence of unpunished illegal government behavior. The first chapter explains this apparent paradox by showing why and how the courts are fundamentally political institutions, tied to the governing elites who make foreign policy in ways that make it unlikely that the courts will accept the CAM's legal arguments.

The second chapter examines the constitutional aspects of the executive branch's warmaking activities. It explains why the Presidency has taken the leading role in formulating foreign policy since the end

Box Two

A Short Course in Jurisprudence

Justice Oliver Wendell Holmes gave a speech in 1897 that many lawyers have taken to heart. In the speech, Holmes said, "If you want to know the law and nothing else, you must look at it as a bad man, who cares only for the material consequences which such knowledge enables him to predict." An early Wall Street lawyer had a discussion with a client in which this "bad man" theory of the law was stated in a different way. The client said, "I don't want you to tell me why I *can't* do what I want to do; I want you to tell me *how* to do it." This way of thinking about the law—that the law is nothing more than the limit on what you can get away with—is controversial but quite influential. Indeed, it probably describes the ordinary thinking of lawyers in their everyday work. It also accounts for the almost spontaneous way that lawyers can make it seem that language in statutes—language that a nonlawyer would think was absolutely clear—is actually ambiguous. The discussions of the Boland Amendment during the Iran-contra hearings illustrate the "bad man" theory of the law in operation.

The version of the Boland Amendment that was the focus of these discussions provided that "no funds available to the Central Intelligence Agency, the Department of Defense, or any other agency or entity of the United States involved in intelligence activities may be...expended for the purpose...of supporting, directly or indirectly, military or paramilitary operations in Nicaragua by any nation, group, organization, movement, or individual." The hearings established that Colonel Oliver North of the staff of the National Security Council did support the contras directly and indirectly, using United States government funds.

Most people reading the Boland Amendment probably thought that Colonel North's activities violated the Amendment. After all, it seems clear that he was "involved in intelligence activities" and had supported the contras. Those who defended his activities countered that the National Security Council was not an "agency or entity of the United States involved in intelligence activities." One of their better arguments was that the term "agency or entity" refers to organizations that are authorized by statute to engage in intelligence activities—a sort of bureaucratic definition. The National Security Council is not an intelligence agency of that sort; it is composed of Cabinet-level officials who advise the President based on information coordinated by the Council's staff. Defenders of the administration's activities contended that, in light of the differences between the National Security Council and other intelligence agencies, the Boland Amendment simply didn't apply to Colonel North.

A second line of defense was that, if the Boland Amendment did apply, it was unconstitutional. According to this argument, the National

---

Security Council and its staff are personal advisers to the President, and just as Congress could not prohibit the *President* from personally supporting the contras—by giving them direct or indirect political support—it can't prohibit the President's personal staff from doing so.

Neither of these arguments are conclusive, of course. The Boland Amendment might be interpreted to adopt a functional, not a bureaucratic, definition of "agency or entity"—that is, if someone is *doing* the activity referred to in the Amendment, that person is covered by it. And it's easy to see that we don't have to treat the large staff of the National Security Council as the direct extension of the President's personal activities.

The point of the "bad man" theory of the law, though, is that if we haven't pinned down every possible escape hatch and loophole, "the law" actually does not prohibit what the "bad man" wants to do.

of World War II, and why Congress has not resisted the expansion of Presidential power.

The third chapter considers the constitutional law regarding civil liberties in the context of warmaking. Particularly with respect to civil liberties issues, people often think that the law and the courts are neutral and nonpolitical—the law has rules to ensure that whatever government does is fundamentally fair and decent, and the courts enforce those rules evenhandedly. This chapter shows that this view overlooks important dimensions of the problem. For example, it assumes that we can distinguish between "the courts" and "the government," yet, as we will see, the courts are part of the government, which affects the way they enforce the law. At the same time, though, important popular traditions find support in the law for claims that government policies are illegal no matter what the courts say.

The fourth chapter examines those traditions and their use by the CAM. It shows why it sometimes makes sense for the CAM to assert as vigorously as possible its arguments about the illegality of United States policy—not simply to persuade courts (which may sometimes happen, but often won't), but also to draw upon the public's sense of fairness and its desire to see that its government operates legally.

This pamphlet has three themes. First, the Constitution, as interpreted by the courts and because of its fundamental structure, does provide support for arguments that current United States are illegal, but it provides equally firm support for arguments that those policies are completely legal. For this reason, law is a terrain of political contention. Sometimes we can understand law best by seeing it as the reflection of divisions among ruling elites, or between ruling elites and popular opposition. Sometimes these divisions are reflected in formal divisions in the institutions of government. For example, Chapter Two examines the consequences of the separation of powers in the United States government; the existence of a Congress separate from the Presidency means that these two important branches are sometimes controlled by people who have different positions on particular issues. The CAM's ability to use the law in its activities may depend on the degree of this sort of division among political issues. And movement activity may produce reactions among political elites that make it more likely that legal challenges will succeed. Sometimes the divisions among political elites are less formal. Because judges are appointed for life terms (see Box Three), the court system as a whole may reflect changes in the priorities different parts of the political elite give to different elites. The formal institutions of law provide the structures in which political conflicts take place, but they don't resolve those conflicts.

A second theme is that, despite some opportunities opened up by the possibility of using law as a terrain of political contention, a CAM legal strategy that focuses on the courts is unlikely to succeed, if success is defined—as it might be in a purely legalistic strategy—on winning judgments from courts. That's because law can also be understood as maintaining the system by defining the broad boundaries within which political elites reach the compromises that constitute "the system" at any time. In this way, law sets the ground rules for politics, and the courts can interpret those rules to guarantee that things don't get out of hand, from the point of view of people in power.

The third and final theme of the pamphlet develops the distinction between a legal strategy, focused on courts, and the CAM's legal arguments. Those arguments can be part of a political strategy. When political elites disagree, the CAM's legal arguments can provide a way of expressing and multiplying that disagreement. In addition, law to some extent expresses important popular aspirations. Terms like "due process of law" and "equal protection" have entered into the ordinary language of political debate. People can appeal to those concepts and argue that government actions violate them even if the courts have rejected such claims when they are presented in legal cases. Popular aspirations to fairness and justice are captured in our legal language; the CAM can formulate its appeals in that language, and show how United States policy denies those aspirations. The legal system provides opportunities for political activity that can enhance the sense that members of a political movement can use the existing instruments of power in their effort to change existing policy. For example, they can obtain acquittals in criminal cases, which can be publicized to show that

---

Box Three

Law as Politics

Statements about illegality are more than expressions of deep disagreement with United States policy, but they don't capture all the dimensions of disagreement. The CAM is no more satisfied with the "legal" military assistance provided to the contras after the Boland Amendments expired than it was with "illegal" assistance that violated those amendments and the Neutrality Act. The CAM's legal arguments are part of a broader political strategy. Treating law as part of a political strategy may seem inconsistent with widely-held views about the neutrality of law, but those views accept lots of mythology about law. Here's why law isn't neutral:

Law is almost always *unclear*. What does "due process of law" mean?—fair outcomes, fair procedures, traditional procedures, or what? Judges have to decide what legal terms mean. The lack of clarity in legal terms means that judges, trying to do their best in interpreting the law, will have to draw on their understanding of politics, economics, social organization, and the like to arrive at their interpretation of the law. It promotes our understanding of how the courts work to see that those understandings are "political," in a useful sense that doesn't impute crass motivations to the judges.

That's not to say that politics, in a narrower sense, doesn't play some role in legal interpretation. The controversy of "original intent" illustrates this. People like Attorney General Meese say that judges should be limited by the original intent of the drafters of the Constitution. Just about everyone knows that that's just a method for him to inject his political views into the law. Although the intent of the framers is often unclear even about the social problems of their day, the more fundamental difficulty is that we cannot easily transpose their intent into the contemporary world so that it helps us understand our social problems. For example, when the framers thought about problems of religious liberty, they thought that those problems mattered because they posed difficulties for a society composed of adherents of different Protestant denominations. Their understanding of religious liberty was defined by their assumption that their society was, and would continue to be, a Protestant society. Our society is no longer as exclusively Protestant, which makes it extremely difficult—perhaps impossible—to reconstruct the framers' intent in a way that makes it relevant to our different kind of society. In the area of foreign affairs, the framers did not have in mind the distinctive problems rising from the role of the United States as a superpower in an era of nuclear weapons, and their "intent" about the proper relation of President and Congress, again, cannot be very helpful in solving those problems.

Judges are *politicians*. They are appointed by politicians; many were active in politics before they became judges. They don't lose their partisan impulses when they become judges, and the kinds of issues that the CAM raises are especially likely to trigger those impulses. Notice that everyone knows what we mean when we say that Chief Justice Rehnquist is "conservative" and Justice Brennan is "liberal." And we don't mean anything dramatically different from calling Ronald Reagan conservative and Edward Kennedy liberal.

government policies are unpopular, and they can use the information brought out in lawsuits in wider campaigns of political education.

Even so, the limits on law as part of a political strategy always have to be kept in mind. Activists associated with social movements in the past were sometimes so captivated by a legal strategy—one focused on the courts—that they forgot that other strategies might have been more useful. And, more important, movement activists have to expect lots of losses in the courts, which most of the time will be "system maintainers." If activists place too much emphasis on legal strategies focused on the courts, they may lose heart. But if they understand the complex roles of law—and in particular, if movement activists remind themselves that legal arguments can heighten tensions among political elites and can appeal to popular aspirations—they may find legal *arguments* quite useful as one part of an overall political strategy. By understanding how law is one of many ways in which politics is conducted, movement activists may be able to develop a flexible legal and political strategy that takes account of the opportunities that legal strategies present *and* the limitations upon the effectiveness of such strategies.

CHAPTER ONE

The Constitution
and the Courts

Political issues are at the heart of the work of the courts in the United States. In other countries, questions about things like public assistance and foreign policy are heatedly debated by contending political parties and are resolved by elections. The policy the legislature and executive approve goes into effect. In the United States these and similar issues are routinely presented to the courts, and people tend to think that an issue is not resolved until the courts decide whether it is constitutional or not. This chapter examines the sources of the unusual "court and law" focus of United States politics. It has its origins in some historical and cultural aspects of United States politics, as well as in some of the premises of the organization of the United States government.

The Law-Centered Politics
of the United States

Law is a set of rules that define and provide structure to our daily interactions with each other, and similarly define and structure the political system. It has its own specific methods of operating, and some characteristic ways of presenting and dealing with arguments, but it is still a form of politics. Equally important, law interacts with politics. We can't escape the problems of politics by moving into the legal system, but we can use that system to highlight political conflicts. The history and culture of the United States, as well as the structure of the government, explain why law plays such an important role in United States politics.

The United States Revolution was in large measure the result of a disagreement about the fundamental structure of organizing political power—that is, about the issues that we now deal with in the United States Constitution. Many colonists believed that they should have the ultimate power to determine the policies that governed their lives and especially their economic activities. Most people in the British government were willing to concede that on many matters it made sense to let the colonists decide what to do. But the prevailing view in the British government was that they had the lawful authority to impose their policies on the colonists, even if they didn't do that very often. From the beginning, then, United States politics took the form of a dispute about fundamental law—again in present-day terms, constitutional law.

The deeply embedded Protestant culture of the United States led people to draw their morality from a specific text, the Bible. Protestantism meant that each individual could claim as great authority for his or her personal understanding of the Bible as anyone else. There were no priests to interpret the Bible in a definitive way. This attitude toward "texts" was easily transferred to the law. In particular, the Constitution became something like a secular Bible. The Protestant culture led many people to resist claims that the legislature or even the Supreme Court could determine for everyone what the Constitution meant. Protestants believed that the Bible meant what it said, and didn't need anyone to tell them what it meant. Similarly, people in the United States often believe that they don't need anyone to tell them what the Constitution means. This contributes to a political culture in which people are reluctant to take any issue as settled. If they have the chance, they will reopen an issue in another forum. And they don't have to wait until the next election because the courts are always available to them.

Another important source of the law focus of United States politics is the structure of government. Political bargaining occurs within boundaries set by a system of rules that organize politics. In the United States the Constitution embodies those rules. The fundamental problem that the Constitution addresses is that its framers wanted to create a relatively powerful centralized government but were also concerned that the power of the central government might be used to interfere with what they thought valuable—in particular, with the ability of people to engage in productive economic activity within a stable political environment. They believed that they could not have a powerful centralized government that was also completely democratic because popular forces would be able to take over the central government and use it to alter the distribution of the products of economic activity.

The Constitution resulted from dissatisfaction among important political elites with the operation of the Articles of Confederation that had guided the "national" government after the end of the Revolution. The Articles of Confederation created a government that was essentially an alliance among independent states. It could act only if the states unanimously agreed. Not surprisingly, it was hard to get that agreement on contentious issues. In addition, the Confederation could not raise money on its own; it could merely request that the states tax their people to raise money for an army and other national activities. As a result of the weakness of the Confederation, merchants who were involved in international trade found themselves unable to overcome local legislation that made it hard for them to compete, and unable as well to develop a national program to support a credit system that could attract capital investment in the new nation. In addition, farming interests, especially in the South, wanted to participate actively in world markets, but needed a stable credit system to finance their activities. Even farmers who were less concerned about producing for world markets believed that a more powerful government could promote economic activity in ways that would ultimately assist them.

Many creditors were also worried about what they saw as excesses of democracy at the local level. State governments relieved debtors of their legal obligation to repay loans. In the winter of 1786-87, an armed uprising in Western Massachusetts closed the courts that creditors used to collect debts.[1] Farmers and workers in small crafts workshops, although they too tended to support expansive economic growth, were sensitive to the instability that growth caused, as the uncontrolled operation of markets produced unexpected losses those farmers and workers. They therefore desired a relatively more democratic government, which, to them, meant one that was less centralized than the one that many creditors and owners of larger farms and plantations desired. Yet, even the latter were committed to a government in which there was more popular participation than had been the case under British rule.

The framers of the Constitution, who met in Philadelphia in the summer of 1787, wanted to "improve" the government by making it easier to obtain national action to support economic growth, by making it harder for local majorities to inhibit those national interests, and by assuring that the nation would be strong enough to honor its international obligations and to act—or to provide a model that other nations could imitate—in international affairs. These desires might have led the framers to create a powerful, unified national government, which is indeed what James Madison wanted. Yet, many people in the states, such as the smaller farmers and artisans, were understandably suspicious of efforts to deprive them of the power to rule that they had fought for in the Revolution. This made it politically impossible to create a powerful centralized government.

But that sort of government was troubling even to people like Madison. They were committed, as a matter of principle and in response to practical realities, to a system of government in which popular participation played a major role—in short, to a relatively democratic system of government. This created a problem for the supporters of a strong centralized government who were concerned about excesses of democracy in the states. Once a national government was created, they couldn't be sure that it would not be taken over by the very democratic forces that they worried about in the states. The farmers and artisans who promoted "instability" in some states might form a coalition on the national level that would use the power of the centralized government to undo or modify contracts, insulate them from the surprises of an unregulated market, and the like.

Drawing on their experiences and interpretations of political theory, the drafters of the Constitution devised an ingenious solution to their problems. They created a national government that had substantial *authority* to act, but made it difficult for that government to exercise its authority. The Constitution's supporters believed that they could get the national government to act on their behalf—for example, by forcing states to eliminate restrictions on interstate trade and by creating a national credit system—while making it hard for their democratic adversaries to capture the government. The framers accomplished these goals through the overall structure of the government they created.

One part of the solution to the problem of combining centralization with protection for economic activity was to create a federal system. The central government would be authorized to take a great deal of action but it would be organized so that popular forces would find it quite difficult to gain control of it. Congress was created with two branches, each elected in a different way (popular election of the Senate was not adopted until 1913), and for different terms. The President was elected in another, indirect way and had the power to veto legislation. And ultimately the courts could hold laws unconstitutional.

The division of authority between the states and the central government contributed to the development of a politics focused on

Box Four

The Court System

There are two court systems in the United States. *State* courts deal with most ordinary lawsuits and criminal cases. When people are arrested at demonstrations, for example, against CIA recruiting, they will usually be prosecuted in state courts. The Constitution requires that state courts consider any constitutional claims defendants make—for example, that the demonstration was protected by freedom of speech. The Constitution also requires that state courts consider well-founded defenses based on international law. If these claims are rejected in the state courts, defendants can appeal to higher state courts, and ultimately to the Supreme Court. Judges in most states are elected, which makes them sensitive to local political concerns. Obviously, this can sometimes help CAM activists, for example, those who demonstrate in cities with a strong CAM presence; and it can sometimes hurt them, for example, those who demonstrate in cities where there is strong support for intervention in Central America. In general, though, state courts are not likely to be important to the CAM.

Because the CAM is concerned with the foreign policy of the national government, most of its involvement with the courts will be with the national (usually called *federal*) courts. CAM activists may try to block expenditures on activities in Central America (an *injunction*). They may try to recover *damages* from CIA or FBI agents who conducted break-ins at their offices. They may become defendants in cases charging violations of immigration laws.

The lowest level of the federal court system is the *district court.* A single district judge decides cases first; in criminal cases and most damage suits the judge must also use a jury. Trial judges have a lot of control over how a lawsuit proceeds. They rule on the admissibility of evidence, help expand or limit the amount of information one side can get from the other before trial occurs (called *discovery*), and speed up or slow down the pace of a lawsuit. In many cases against the national government, they also decide which side's claims about the facts to believe; sometimes, as in criminal prosecutions, juries decide the facts, but special rules limit the jury's role in suits against the government.

Decisions by a district judge are reviewed by the *courts of appeals* for the area. There are thirteen courts of appeals, one a specialized court, one for the District of Columbia, and eleven for regional groups of states. Each court of appeals has several judges, ranging from six to over twenty. These courts sit in groups of three, drawn randomly from the entire court of appeals. (In special cases, a court of appeals will sit *en banc,* which means that all of the judges participate in the decision.) The courts of appeals basically decide only questions of law, taking as given the facts that the district judge found.

> The Supreme Court reviews decisions by the courts of appeals. It has almost complete control over deciding which cases to review. In most cases, the Court simply refuses to review the decisions of the courts of appeals, letting those decisions stand without directly approving them. This lets the Court stay out of controversial areas, if it wants to, until a national consensus on the issues emerges.
>
> All federal judges are nominated by the President and confirmed by the Senate. They serve for life terms. Presidents nominate people who share their general political views, and in recent years the Reagan administration has taken great care to assure that the judges it appoints are quite conservative. The Senate rarely refuses to confirm a judge that the administration nominates; the confirmation process can do little more than make the judges, taken as a group, very slightly less conservative (or liberal) than the administration might prefer.

law. In the basic scheme of the Constitution, most economic activity would be regulated by state governments, but the Constitution prevented them from adopting "disruptive" economic policies. For example, they could not issue paper money or enact statutes relieving debtors of their contractual obligations to creditors.

Federalism had deep effects on politics in the United States. James Madison understood that in a federal system that occupied a large territory, popular forces would find it difficult to organize. Economic dislocation that affected one region might not affect others at the same time, and it might subside within the four or six years needed to gain control of Congress and the Presidency. In the nineteenth century, sheer distance also made it hard for people in different states to coordinate their political programs. These factors helped create the particular structure of political parties in the United States. From their beginnings in the early 1800s through the nineteenth century, the so-called national political parties were much more like alliances among local political groups than they were unified organizations with a common political program.

The local focus of politics in the United States contributed to the development of a law-centered politics. As alliances of local groups, the national parties could do little more than cut deals to get the national government to adopt policies that would let local economic forces have their way. In many ways that was precisely what the framers had intended. The effect was that until the end of the nineteenth century the national government encouraged and subsidized local economic development but did not regulate it. Rather, any regulation occurred on the local level. Regulation took two forms. Sometimes state legislatures enacted statutes imposing limits on economic activity. Even

TABLE ONE

Judges on the federal courts, 1987, by appointing President

District Courts

Reagan	213 (40%)
Carter	199 (38%)
Nixon-Ford	92 (17%)
Other (mostly Johnson-Kennedy)	26 (5%)

Courts of Appeals

Reagan	63 (41%)
Carter	52 (34%)
Nixon-Ford	25 (16%)
Other	14 (9%)

For the near future, the federal courts will be staffed by judges appointed by several Presidents.

Slightly less than half will have been appointed by President Carter, whose judges tended to be centrist liberals. About half will be Reagan appointees, with a slightly higher concentration of Reagan appointees in the courts of appeals. A lot of what happens in the lower federal courts will depend on the luck of the draw. If a CAM case comes before a Carter appointee, it has better prospects than otherwise. It is much harder to get a favorable panel in the courts of appeals, where the Reagan appointees have begun to constitute a majority.

these statutes had to survive judicial attention: the courts had to interpret the statutes and uphold them before regulation would take effect. And, as economic development proceeded, the mobility of capital meant that investors troubled by the regulations imposed in one location could move to another that would be willing to let them operate without complying with public regulation.

The second form of regulation was more important in creating a law-focused politics. This form used the courts, not the legislatures, to regulate economic activity. Courts did so by defining what counted as a property right in a rapidly changing economy, by determining what sorts of contracts should be enforced, and by developing the rules regarding the liability of manufacturers for the injuries caused by their activities.[2] For example, as the technology of power generation developed, owners of land on rivers sometimes dammed the rivers to create new power sources. Although this helped new industries, it deprived landowners downstream of water that they had used to irrigate their farms. Had the upstream owners violated the property rights of the downstream ones? (At first courts and legislatures tended to say Yes, and then as industry became more important they tended to say No.) Or, suppose an employer hired a worker for a year and promised to pay the wages at the end. If the worker left after six months, because the employer was abusive or because there were better opportunities elsewhere, should the worker get half of the promised wages? (Most of the courts said No.) What matters here for our purposes is that the disgruntled downstream farmer or the disgruntled former worker did not have to get a political party to back their complaints. Their problems presented ordinary problems of property and contract law. Everybody knew that courts were supposed to decide those cases.

Law became the focus of politics in the United States then because the structure of the national government forced the most important issues to the local level, because local and national political parties sought to encourage economic development by keeping their hands off private actors, and because courts had to resolve fundamental issues arising from economic growth in the course of deciding traditional lawsuits.

The Separation of Powers, Sustained Agreement, and Foreign Policy

The "separation of powers" is the second important structural feature of the United States government. Separation of powers means that there are several branches in the national government, each of which has certain powers and each of which can exercise those powers only in a complex interaction with the other branches. Some examples centering on foreign policy are these: The Constitution gives Congress the power to declare war and "provide for the common defense"; Congress also appropriates money for the armed forces. The President has the "executive" power, and is commander-in-chief of the armed forces; the President also makes treaties with the advice and consent of the Senate. The separation of powers, like federalism, was designed to respond to the desire for a national government that was both strong and unthreatening to private economic activity. The separation of powers means that the United States government is able to act most easily when there is sustained agreement among political elites. (We will see that modern conditions give the President a special ability to initiate action, particularly in foreign policy. The long-term success of those initiatives requires that agreement develop.) We can use the idea of sustained agreement to examine in somewhat greater detail the structure of the national government as it affects the development of United States foreign policy.

By creating these different governing institutions, the Constitution set up a system in which, as Madison put it, "ambition [would] counteract ambition."[3] This idea is sometimes also described as "checks and balances"—each branch can get what it wants only if the other branches agree not to "check" or limit it. For example, Congress can pass bills, but they will not become enforceable statutes if the President vetoes them unless Congress "overrides" the veto by a two-thirds vote in both the House of Representatives and the Senate. Congress has the power to initiate legislation, but its power is checked by the President's veto power, which is in turn limited by Congress's power to override the veto.

Separation of powers leads to substantial bargaining between the President and Congress. Today, for example, the President proposes a budget that embodies his plans for further military buildups. The Congress counters with a budget bill that limits the growth of military spending and increases taxes. In the end, they strike a deal and seek political approval from the voters for what they did and tried to do. Congressional committees hold hearings on administration activities, where members of the administration defend in public what they have done.

The framers assumed that Congress would be the primary actor in developing national policy, foreign as well as domestic. But the strength of Congress would be balanced by a strong executive branch. The government would then be strong enough to do what was important, but could not be turned against the interests the framers valued. The courts had a rather small role in this scheme; they were to maintain the general outlines of the system that separated the activities of Congress from those of the President, but within those outlines President and Congress would make deals that each believed would serve its interests. The courts would leave these deals essentially untouched. For example, the courts have almost nothing to say about the distribution of expenditures and taxes in the national budget, and they have almost never supervised the manner in which Congress conducts its legislative hearings into the administration of the laws.

The Constitution contained an unavoidable tension, though. The framers wanted a national government that could act vigorously in domestic and foreign affairs, but not too vigorously. Every counter-balancing institution that protected against overreaching also made it harder to accomplish anything. Vigorous action might be forthcoming if somehow the competing interests were coordinated, but how could that be done without losing the benefits of "counteracting ambition"? If there is a solution to this problem in the structure of the Constitution, it arises from the system of staggered elections. Presidents are elected every four years; members of the House of Representatives serve two-year terms, and Senators serve six-year terms. Coordinated action can occur if elite support for a governing coalition holds together long enough to put people in the House, the Senate, and the Presidency who agree on what should be done. That is, a sustained agreement among political elites will guarantee vigorous action, while more transitory—and, the framers assumed, more democratic—impulses could not be acted on.

In one sense, the system the framers created has worked exactly as they expected. The government has implemented the sustained agreement of political elites on foreign policy since 1945. Of course, the framers envisioned much less foreign involvement than has actually occurred, but they created a Constitution that could and did enable activities they did not specifically have in mind. What they wanted was a government that would act vigorously when there was sustained agreement supporting action, and that's what they got.

Agreement has been sustained in two important ways. A national party system developed soon after the Constitution was adopted. Originally the national parties were rather temporary alliances among local politicians, but they have evolved into relatively coherent groups of people who pretty much think alike on many important issues. Political allegiance to a party's program—or even the simple desire to see their party win—provides a degree of coordination among Representatives, Senators, and Presidents or presidential candidates.

The parties are not completely unified on all issues, or on details of policies on which they are generally agreed. The parties collect people into two broad-based, national groups. These groups could be sharply distinct from each other: A Democratic administration might immediately reverse the policies adopted by a Republican predecessor. At least in foreign policy, that doesn't happen. Foreign policy is an arena of sustained agreement because the twentieth century has seen the United States become one of the leading world powers. Until relatively recently, the United States role in international affairs conferred substantial economic benefits on most politically active segments of United States society. Under those circumstances, people troubled by the United States activities abroad would have to overcome the inertia that was produced by the benefits of those activities. That made it difficult—until recently—to develop substantial popular opposition to United States foreign policy, which is to say that there has been general agreement on the United States role in foreign affairs. As part of that consensus, political elites have come to agree that, on the whole, "politics stops at the water's edge." They believe that it is usually more important to support the President's program, whatever it is, than to make sure that it is the right program. Further, political elites have shared a deep agreement that the interests of the United States were best served by a strong stance in opposition to the expansion of the influence of the Soviet Union. That agreement allowed vigorous action to be taken, though sometimes there was disagreement over the best way to implement that agreement.[4]

The next chapter discusses the roles of the President and Congress in making and implementing foreign policy within the limits of this ideology. For purposes of this overview, it is enough to note here that the development of modern forms of war-making in the nuclear era have given the President more power to initiate action than Congress. The ideology of anti-Communism and the technology of nuclear weapons have promoted the further development of a system of secrecy in the area of foreign affairs: Foreign policy elites believe it important to conceal lots of information about weaponry and foreign affairs from Soviet spies, which leads to concealing much of that information, and more, from Congress and the public. Secrecy enhances the President's power, because he can always try to justify his initiatives by saying that he has secret information. These claims can later be challenged, but by then momentum and the ideology of standing behind the President will have changed the political posture of the policy.

Taken together, these aspects of the constitutional structure, coupled with the role of the United States in the contemporary world, allow the President to initiate quite substantial and often controversial foreign policy programs. That degree of vigor may not have been what the framers had in mind, particularly because such initiatives may threaten democratic values in the United States and—less important to the framers—elsewhere. The third branch in the constitutional structure—the court system—can be one way to handle this sort of threat.

Initially, the courts were important because the Constitution limited the powers of state governments, and the framers wanted to guarantee that those limitations would be respected. For example, the framers' fear of laws relieving debtors led them to include in the Constitution a ban on any state laws "impairing the obligation of contracts." Later, during the effort to get the Constitution adopted, opponents of the Constitution insisted that other specific limitations be placed on the national government in the Bill of Rights. All of these limitations were supposed to be enforced by the courts. Even if Congress and the President agreed to act, the courts—in theory—would stop them when their acts violated the limits the Constitution placed on them.

The Courts and Civil Liberties in Overview

When people think about the Supreme Court, cases like the desegregation decisions and the abortion decisions probably come first to mind. The popular image is of a Supreme Court whose primary job is protecting civil liberties. And indeed sometimes people can use the courts to advance their political goals. For example, the civil rights movement of the 1950s and 1960s was able to take advantage of the fact that the South's overtly racist policies were rejected by most of the rest of the country's political elite. They called on the national courts to enforce something like a national consensus against segregation in opposition to regional support for it. But when the civil rights movement turned to issues like housing discrimination, it found the courts less receptive precisely because the governing elites were more divided over the wisdom of extensive efforts to combat that sort of discrimination. As a result, there was no nationwide agreement on what should be done that the courts could assist.

The civil rights example shows how a social movement can sometimes use the courts to help it achieve its goals. Sometimes the courts can help a movement resist oppression by other branches of the government. For example, the antiwar movement of the 1960s and 1970s was able to raise the cost of oppression substantially by forcing prosecutors and other executive officials to justify in court what they were trying to do. These efforts were not completely successful. But whatever success they had was due, once again, to the existence of divisions within the governing elites over the wisdom both of the war in Vietnam and of the effort to suppress dissent in the United States.

When social movements use the courts to promote civil liberties they are acting to exploit and intensify divisions among political elites. They can do that, though, because civil liberties law is the primary embodiment of the aspirational elements in United States law. It became that embodiment over the course of a long and complex history that culminated with the development of a real law of civil liberties in the twentieth century.[5]

The story goes back at least to the Magna Carta in 1215, when wealthy feudal lords in England forced King John to accept limitations on the exercise of what they regarded as arbitrary royal power. The Magna Carta is usually taken as the first expression in Anglo-American law of the idea that we should have "a government of laws and not a government of men." A government of men is one in which arbitrary power could be exercised by whoever happens to hold it, while a government of laws is one whose exercises of power can always be brought into question through the ordinary operations of courts. For example, early English law developed the writ of habeas corpus. That writ still allows people who are arrested by the police to call on the courts to force the police to explain why the arrests are justified. One only has to think about the prevalence of "disappearances" in Central American dictatorships to understand the importance of a system in which habeas corpus is routinely available; the restoration of habeas corpus was one of the first acts taken after the overthrow of the military regime in Argentina.

The example of habeas corpus illustrates the interaction between elite disagreements and popular movements. Habeas corpus originated in the struggle between feudal lords and the King. Eventually it became a fundamental guarantee of civil liberty for everyone. How did that happen? As usual, the story is quite complicated. In its main outlines it involves repeated challenges by elites to the exercise of arbitrary royal power. As merchants and capitalists began to gain economic power in England they discovered that the traditional system of law obstructed the conduct of their activities. They had enough power, deriving from their ability to finance the operations of government, to extract concessions from the king, though they did not have enough military power to displace the monarchy entirely. They explained their objections to royal rule not simply in terms of their economic self-interest, but also in the terms of "the rule of law." That is, they developed and promulgated an ideology according to which arbitrary government was both bad for business and bad for the people. That ideology was widely popularized, for the new capitalists understood that, carefully controlled, the people could be important allies in their struggle against arbitrary royal power. Yet, once the ideology was popularized, it fueled popular movements to extend civil liberties. After all, if freedom from arbitrary rule was good for capitalists, why wasn't it good for everyone?

Of course it was hard to spell out what "arbitrary government" meant. The most important early element in the definition of civil liberties was the right to vote. In the colonies that became the United States, the relatively equal distribution of property—compared to that in England—made it fairly easy to establish the right of all white males to vote by 1800 or so. Abolitionists and proponents of women's suffrage repeatedly used the arbitrariness of white rule and of men's control as an important argument for their positions, thereby drawing on the ideology of the rule of law to support their political claims.

The idea of civil liberties emerged in the interaction between elite divisions and popular movements. As suffrage was extended, the popular majority—limited as it was—insisted that the benefits that had been claimed by some among the elite, should be extended to more of the people. They were sometimes successful because elites were, after all, divided, because some in the political elite found it sensible to build alliances with popular movements, and because those movements had enough power on their own to made it almost necessary for the elites to reach some sort of accommodation with the movements. The effect in the end was to write into law phrases that expressed popular aspirations to justice.

The Bill of Rights provides a good example of this process. As we have seen, the Constitution proposed by the Convention of 1787 was quite concerned about the possibility of democratic "excesses" like debtor relief laws. And indeed the Antifederalists—the name given to those who opposed the ratification of the Constitution—repeatedly attacked it as antidemocratic, and as making it possible for a centralized government controlled by an elite to oppress the people. The Antifederalists had a lot of support; immediately after the Convention, majorities in perhaps seven states opposed the ratification of the Constitution. The men who wanted to have the Constitution adopted knew that they had to allay at least some of the Antifederalist concerns. James Madison, who was a superb politician as well as a profound political theorist, adopted the strategy of promising the Antifederalists that the first Congress elected under the new Constitution would propose a Bill of Rights. That promise, which Madison of course honored, swung the vote to adopt the Constitution in several crucial states.

Constitutional provisions like habeas corpus and the Bill of Rights allow the courts to protect civil liberties against arbitrary exercises of power. But the courts still have to decide whether a government action, challenged as arbitrary, really was arbitrary. The limitations that the Constitution places on government do not define themselves. For example, the courts have to *decide* whether prosecuting Sanctuary supporters violates the constitutional guarantee of free exercise of religion. The courts have developed complex legal standards to guide their decisions, some of which are discussed in Chapter Three. But those standards don't come just from the words of the Constitution. They also come from the judges' response to their circumstances. Those circumstances include the historical situation and some aspects of the structure of the Constitution that have not yet been discussed.

The influence of *historical circumstances* is shown in the history of civil liberties law. Consider three episodes in that history.

1. Property rights

The rule of law means that the courts should keep the government from acting arbitrarily. From 1895 to 1937, the Supreme Court allied itself with established property interests and struck down progressive laws, such as minimum wage and maximum hours laws, supported by the labor movement.[6] Historians explain the Court's action by noting that, though union supporters had gained some power in some state legislatures, they had not built national support for that degree of regulation of business. When such support was created during the Depression and the New Deal, the Court came into line and repudiated its earlier definition of what was arbitrary government power. The Court's actions from 1895 to 1937 amounted to a political intervention in a fluid political climate, making it easier for the propertied classes to prevail. Interestingly, the Court has recently revived its interest in interpreting the Constitution to protect capital against public regulation, including legislation aimed at alleviating the effects of plant closings.[7] Once again, the Court's role in aiding one side in struggles that remain unresolved in the national political process is evident.

2. Free speech

The courts did little to protect free speech in the early years of the twentieth century.[8] The Industrial Workers of the World (the "Wobblies") were driven off public platforms and jailed for making speeches urging workers to join unions and strike. The Supreme Court upheld the prosecutions of radicals for making "seditious" speeches—that is, speeches severely critical of the capitalist system and urging action to replace it. Only when unions gained strength and became part of the Democratic Party coalition during the New Deal did the Court begin to develop a theory of free speech that actually protected dissidents. And when the Court led by Chief Justice Earl Warren advanced the cause of civil liberties in the 1960s, it continued the work of the New Deal coalition; the liberals who were the New Deal's constituency became the Court's.[9]

3. Desegregation

In 1954, the Supreme Court held that school segregation was unconstitutional, invalidating laws in all southern states.[10] This disturbed the agreement among southern white elites for segregation, but did so in the service of an emerging national agreement. For example, the federal Department of Justice presented an argument to the Supreme Court in 1947 challenging the constitutionality of state rules allowing property owners to restrict the sale of their property to whites only. The Department noted the criticism of racial discrimination that "those with competing philosophies" had made "throughout the world."[11] Segregation was embarrassing the conduct of United States foreign policy, providing the Soviet Union with ammmunition for its charge that capitalism was socially regressive. Both parties believed that support from northern blacks would help them.

The *structural features* of the Constitution lead the courts to give its provisions particular meanings for reasons like the ones that lead to agreement between Congress and the President. Federal judges are appointed by the President, and confirmed by the Senate. This connects them to the political branches of the system. But federal judges serve for life terms, and so at any specific time some judges might be at odds with Congress or the President. Even so, if a political coalition holds power in Congress and the Presidency for a long enough period, it will come to control the courts as well. The courts come to join the sustained agreement that leads to coordinated action, though perhaps somewhat more slowly. The courts are part of the government, and can be influenced by many of the same forces that influence Congress and the President. But, because they usually join the sustained agreement on matters of foreign policy, the courts are likely to endorse what Congress and the President agree on.

Once again, the open-endedness of the Constitution's language matters here. Judges are people with backgrounds that lead Presidents to appoint them as judges. The judges interpret the Constitution's vague terms in light of their backgrounds. Conservative judges honestly think that "free exercise of religion" means that almost any government interest should prevail over claims of religious liberty, and liberal judges honestly think that it means that only the strongest government interests should prevail; that sort of predisposition is what makes them conservative or liberal in the first place.

Ducking Political Issues

The courts are part of the system of checks and balances. As we have seen, the framers expected the courts to intervene if Congress began to act in excessively "democratic" ways. But the framers also designed a series of checks on the courts. One of the most important of these is the system of appointments (see Box Four) which assures that, over a relatively short period of time, the court system as a whole will probably come into alignment with the political forces that prevail in Congress and the Presidency. The appointment process doesn't place limits on any individual judge, or respond to a single decision. Instead, it affects the court system as a whole.

A second check on the courts does affect single decisions, at least to some extent. The courts don't have any direct power to enforce their judgments. They must rely on the other branches to go along with what they say. Of course, over the years the courts have built up a substantial amount of support from important segments of the political system. The Court's decisions in the first amendment area have been sufficiently supportive of the interests of the large news media, for example, that the media tend to support the Court in whatever else it does. The Court's decisions in areas of women's rights and desegregation, while not nearly as much as those constituencies would like, have nonetheless led them to support the Court as well. Thus, it would be quite costly for Congress or the President to defy the Supreme Court openly. If the stakes were high enough, one could expect that it would happen. But the more important dimension of the "lack of power" check on the courts is that some judges have developed a theory of judicial restraint that is predicated on the fear of defiance. That is, they will interpret the Constitution to authorize what Congress or the President have done unless it is absolutely clear that the Constitution prohibits it. And, according to this theory, they do that not because the majority that supports the Congress is entitled to have its way but because the courts would get into trouble if they held the actions unconstitutional. One aspect of this theory is that judges should not decide certain kinds of cases. Unfortunately, judges following this theory sometimes refuse to provoke confrontations even if one might think that the courts would win them.

The courts have developed doctrines they use to avoid deciding some hard cases. Instead of saying that the President's actions in mining harbors in Nicaragua were illegal, for example, they may say that they have no authority to decide whether those actions were illegal or not. By using these doctrines, the courts can let programs continue without annoying the opponents of the programs by saying that the programs are legal, and without annoying the supporters by saying that the programs are illegal.

The two most important doctrines that let courts avoid issues are called standing and political questions.

1. The standing doctrine says that people can't get courts to decide whether some activity is illegal simply because they want to find out, or because a declaration of illegality would generate political pressure to stop the actions. The doctrine requires that people be "injured" in some relatively concrete ways by the activities—and not just any people, but the very people who are the plaintiffs in the lawsuit.[12] CAM activists have standing to bring a lawsuit charging that their offices were illegally broken into. But they probably don't have standing to bring a lawsuit charging that the Boland Amendment denying funds to the contras was violated, because they will have a hard time showing how they personally were injured by the violation of the Amendment. (Sometimes you can find people who have been injured in the required way, but that often diverts the thrust of the litigation away from the major illegalities and toward less important ones that can be seen to cause the injuries.)

It's easy to be skeptical about the standing doctrine. After all, if we are supposed to have a "government of laws, not men [sic]," why shouldn't any concerned person be able to get the courts to say whether the law has been violated? The standing doctrine indicates the limits of law. It helps the courts duck questions that might force them to confront illegal activities by other parts of the government of which they too are part. That way of putting it shows why the courts have developed the standing doctrine: the doctrine obscures the ways in which courts are parts of the government, and restricts the occasions when they might be forced into confrontations with Congress and the President that they might wish to avoid.

2. The political questions doctrine has the same effect. The formal statement of the doctrine is that the courts won't decide questions that the Constitution explicitly says are to be decided exclusively by the President or Congress.[13] That statement seems to limit the doctrine quite a bit, because very few constitutional provisions really say that only Congress of the President can interpret them. But the courts have used the political questions doctrine more broadly. During the Vietnam War, they used the doctrine to avoid deciding whether the war was unconstitutional because the war had not been declared by Congress.[14] More recently, the Supreme Court refused to decide whether the Constitution, which requires the Senate to approve treaties, also requires the Senate to agree with a President's decision to repudiate a treaty.[15] These examples indicate that the political questions doctrine is often used to avoid deciding whether United States foreign policy is legal.

Doctrines like standing and political questions are quite flexible, as they must be if they are to allow courts to duck hot political issues. In this way they are typical of most doctrines of constitutional law. Often you can't tell from the formal statements of the doctrines whether they will get your case thrown out of court. That flexibility can sometimes work to the advantage of opponents of United States foreign policy. If that policy has become vulnerable in the political arena, for example if it has been attacked by a broad popular movement, the courts may be encouraged to rule on the legal challenges that the movement brings—even if they had been reluctant to do so at an earlier point. Then people who earlier did not have standing may find that, under the flexible standing doctrine, they now have it—even though what has changed is not their identity, but the political climate.

The Constitution creates a government that operates according to a theory of sustained agreement. Courts are usually part of that agreement. The Constitution itself therefore places some limits on the effectiveness of court-centered political strategies even as it has contributed to a political culture in which law plays a central role.

CHAPTER TWO

The Imperial Presidency

The Constitution was written when the United States was weak in comparison with countries like England and France. Its authors tended to be suspicious of United States involvement with foreign nations. They feared that the United States could be drawn into military adventures that it could not win. They believed that the best system of international relations was one of free trade among nations. They thought that such a system would guarantee peace by tying competing nations together with bonds of trade that they would not want to threaten by engaging in war; not so incidentally, it would also strengthen the United States, because, the framers believed, the natural and human resources of the country were so great that the United States would inevitably become a major economic force in world trade.

These views led the framers to emphasize Congress's role in foreign affairs. Congress was given the power to declare war and to regulate foreign commerce. Both powers were central to the framers' understanding of what mattered in foreign affairs. Less important, but suggestive of the framers' mindset, the Constitution says that appropriations for the army can't be for "a longer term than two years." In contrast, the President's role was relatively limited. The Constitution makes the President commander-in-chief of the armed forces, a term that suggests control over battlefield operations but not over broader military policy. In addition, the President can "make treaties," but only with the concurrence of the Senate.

The general approach the Constitution takes to foreign policy is fairly clear. As in domestic affairs, Congress is supposed to be the primary actor. But the language of the Constitution doesn't foreclose Presidents from claiming a larger role. For example, Congress has to declare war, but maybe the President can initiate military activities that

TABLE TWO

United States Military Actions Overseas and Congressional Action

Declared wars: 5

War of 1812
Mexican War, 1846
Spanish-American War, 1898
World War I
World War II

Undeclared wars (to 1970): 15

Before 1903:	With France, 1798-1800
	With Tripoli, 1801-05
	Second Barbary War, 1815
1900-40:	Boxer Rebellion, 1900
	Panama, 1903
	Mexico, 1914-17
	Expeditions to Russia, 1918-20
	Nicaragua, 1926-33
	China, 1927
1940-1970:	Pre-war moves, 1939-41
	Korea, 1950-53
	Lebanon, 1958
	Thailand, 1961-70
	Dominican Republic, 1965
	Vietnam, 1964-73

fall short of war, as that term was understood in the 1780s. Maybe the President, as commander-in-chief, can develop military plans that are, in his judgment, appropriate ways to preclude later involvement in war.

The open-endedness of terms like "commander in chief" in the Constitution was intentional. The Constitution did not sharply define the boundaries between what Congress could do and what the President could do. Instead, as we have seen, it established a political system in which the President and Congress would fight each other for power. The hope was that, with ambition counteracting ambition, the best policies would result. Real fights would show that the United States as a whole was divided over what the best policy was, and in such fights neither side would get all that it wanted, thus bringing the outcome closer to what people agreed on. If Congress and the President

Table Two Continued

State Department list of hostile operations overseas prior to 1967:

Actions for which congressional authorization was claimed	7
Naval self-defense	1
Enforcement of law against piracy	8
Landings to protect citizens, prior to 1862	13
Landings to protect citizens, 1865-1967	56
Invasion of foreign or disputed territory, no combat	10
Invasion of foreign or disputed territory, with combat	10
Reprisals against "aborigines"	9
Other reprisals not authorized by statute	4
"Minatory" demonstrations ("showing the flag")	6
Intervention in Panama	1
Protracted occupation of Caribbean states	6
Actions anticipating World War II	1
Bombing of Laos	1
Korean and Vietnamese Wars	2
Miscellaneous	2
Total	**137**

Source: Background Information on the Use of United States Armed Forces in Foreign Countries, Committee on Foreign Affairs, 91st Congress, 2d Session, 1970.

did not fight, that very agreement showed that the policy they wanted was the best one.

From one point of view, the Constitution has been an enormous success. It provided the legal and political framework for the sustained exploitation of the nation's natural resources within an expansive capitalist economy. Economic power was backed up by the growth of the nation's military force, which was frequently used to protect United States economic interests in Central and South America. The United States moved from the margins of international affairs in the 1790s to a more central place after 1900, and into superpower status after 1945. As a result, the nation's political leaders became less concerned that foreign involvements would lead to wars that would hurt the United States.

The New Role of the President

Agreement on the international role of the United States was precisely the sort of sustained consensus that necessarily underlies vigorous action within the constitutional framework. But the transformation of the international role of the United States has also shifted the terms of the political struggle between Congress and the President.

The Constitution is designed in the expectation that the President and Congress will routinely compete for control over domestic and foreign policy.[1] In the nineteenth century, Congress was generally the predominant branch of government. That was because the most important aspects of foreign policy involved commerce and international trade rather than military action. The United States had few military involvements outside the Western hemisphere, and even in this hemisphere the use of official military force was unusual. The idea that peace and the economic interests of the United States would be promoted by prosperity, led Congress to focus on the promotion of trade by means of subsidies, the creation of an economic infrastructure through a nationwide rail system, and tariffs to raise money and protect new industries. Congress's constitutional power over commerce and trade was clear, and the President could not do much on these issues without Congress's cooperation. The President's advantage lies in his power as commander-in-chief of the armed forces, and at a time when military actions were a relatively small aspect of United States foreign policy, Presidents could not readily use that advantage. But even on military issues, Congress sometimes successfully asserted its power. For example, it overcame George Washington's objections and declared neutrality in various European conflicts in the 1790s. The Supreme Court held that the President needed specific statutory authority to seize the property of enemy aliens during wartime. Sometimes the President prevailed. Thomas Jefferson purchased Louisiana from France without congressional authorization. Presidents frequently sent troops abroad— to fight pirates, to open up the Far East to trade, and the like.

The overall picture for the nineteenth century, nonetheless, shows Congress setting the foreign policy agenda. Usually that agenda was uncontroversial, making severe conflict between Congress and the President unlikely. United States foreign policy in the nineteenth century was designed to assure access for United States goods in foreign markets, to protect the physical security of the United States and the commercial interests of its traders abroad, and—after the Monroe Doctrine was proclaimed in 1823—to sustain United States claims to a special role in this hemisphere. But when disagreement arose over details, Congress usually prevailed.

Congress and the President continue to agree on many aspects of foreign policy. What is relatively new is that, in areas of disagreement, the President now has the primary role in initiating policy and thus defining the terrain over which political struggles with Congress, such as they are, will occur. For example, President Reagan defined the "problem" in Central America as Soviet aggression to which a military response was appropriate. Because that definition was consistent with the consensus on foreign policy that it shared, Congress accepted it, and then tinkered with the details of the military response. Notably, it has not offered a nonmilitary program—even a nonmilitary program designed to combat perceived Soviet aggression—for the region.[2]

Several elements contributed to the shift in power to the President that has occurred during the twentieth century. The most important has already been mentioned: the role of the United States in the post-war superpower competition. That role defined the framework within which the ordinary bargaining of politics occurred. The party system and secrecy have some additional effects.

1. The party system: The ideology of bipartisanship in foreign policy alone would not shift power to the President. But the President always has allies in Congress—the members of the President's party. Either a majority or a substantial minority, these members will tend to support the President. *Their* ambition will not counteract his. The party loyalties of members of Congress thus reduce the ability of Congress to win fights with the President.

2. Secrecy: Most important politicians regard secrecy as a necessity of superpower government in modern times. Again, there may be quarrels over the details. But since World War II there has been a sustained consensus on the need for secrecy in many important areas of foreign policy. For example, even though the Constitution says that a "statement and account" of federal expenditures—a fairly detailed budget—"shall be published from time to time," the budget for the Central Intelligence Agency has never been disclosed since the Agency's creation in 1947. As the chief executive, the President initially receives virtually all of the secret information the government acquires. Congress can put pressure on the President to share the secrets, and has done so successfully on some occasions. But, almost by definition, Congress can't know beforehand which secrets it wants to know. And many members of Congress don't want to know. They agree with the political and military initiatives of the national security state and are perfectly happy to see it operate without their interference. This lets the President initiate actions that are then justified by referring to secret information. Again, the terrain is defined by the President.

The Supreme Court's Decisions

So far we have examined only the politics of the imperial Presidency. That is appropriate because the Constitution makes the distribution of power between the President and Congress primarily a matter of politics. The Supreme Court has occasionally discussed these issues, and its position, especially recently, has strongly supported the President.

The modern doctrine of presidential power in foreign affairs originated in the 1936 case of *United States v. Curtiss-Wright Corp.*[3] Congress had passed a statute that authorized the President to prohibit arms sales to Bolivia if he found that such a prohibition "may contribute to the reestablishment of peace" between Bolivia and Paraguay. At that time, giving the President that kind of relatively unguided authority in domestic affairs might have been unconstitutional. The Supreme Court, in an opinion by Justice George Sutherland (a former Senator), said that foreign affairs were different. The Court emphasized the "important, complicated, delicate, and manifold problems" of foreign affairs, and said that the President was "the sole organ of the federal government in the field of international relations." According to Justice Sutherland, the President had to be free of congressional restriction if "serious embarrassment" was to be avoided. The President's access to confidential information and the need to preserve secrecy meant, to the Court, that Congress had almost no role in foreign affairs.

Curtiss-Wright vastly understated the role of Congress, but its view that the President is the primary actor in the field remains important. (See Box Four.) The Court has continued to endorse enhanced presidential power. Probably the most significant recent decision invalidated legislative vetoes. Legislative vetoes were devices that Congress came up with as part of its continuing struggle with the President to control policy. After 1932, Congress found that it could not keep up with public demands for legislative action. Instead of making policy itself, Congress began to write statutes that specified some general goals—like "reestablishing peace" in the Curtiss-Wright case—and left it to administrative agencies or members of the executive branch to work out the details. Sometimes, though, Congress knew that the details mattered a lot. Even though it couldn't work out the details itself, it wanted to keep some control over the results. What Congress did was to add a method of supervision to the delegation of power to executive officials. Congress let the officials make the policy, but it said that the policy wouldn't go into effect if Congress disapproved. These dis-

Box Five

The Curtiss-Wright Case

During the Iran-contra hearings, Colonel Oliver North and his supporters repeatedly referred to the Curtiss-Wright case as a firm statement by the Supreme Court that the Constitution gave the President the predominant role in foreign affairs, and, indeed, that sometimes the President could exclude Congress from participating in making or supervising foreign policy. As with all interpretations of the Constitution, this one resolves ambiguities in the case law in order to advance a particular political position.

Curtiss-Wright does indeed say that "participation in the exercise of the [foreign affairs] power is significantly limited," and that "in this vast external realm, with its important, complicated, delicate and manifold problems, the President alone has the power to speak or listen as a representative of the nation." Justice Sutherland called the President the "sole organ of the federal government in the field of international relations" who had "the very delicate, plenary and exclusive power...which does not require as a basis for its exercise an act of Congress."

How might a defender of Congress respond to claims that *Curtiss-Wright* says that, according to the correct interpretation of the Constitution, Congress must yield to the President in the area of foreign affairs? The facts of *Curtiss-Wright* are the place to begin. The defendant's claim there was that Congress has given away too much of its power to the President. That is, in *Curtiss-Wright* there was no conflict between President and Congress over what the foreign policy of the United States should be. The expansive discussion of the President's exclusive power was irrelevant to the resolution of the case.

In a later case the Supreme Court considered the constitutionality of President Harry Truman's seizure of the steel industry during the Korean War. Truman acted to avert a strike that in his judgment would impair the production of a vital resource during an armed conflict. The Supreme Court held that the seizure was unconstitutional. Several Justices wrote opinions supporting that holding, and each opinion emphasized that President Truman was acting in direct conflict with a direction by Congress that seizure was not permissible. In the most influential opinion, Justice Robert Jackson wrote that the President's power is "at its lowest ebb" when "the President takes measures incompatible with the expressed or implied will of Congress."

According to the Steel Seizure case, the President may have some modest powers that can be exercised even when Congress directs otherwise. But those powers have not been defined by the Supreme Court with any precision. What is clear is that the law, as it is today, does not confirm the strong statements made in the Curtiss-Wright case.

> *Curtiss-Wright* and the Steel Seizure case illustrate again one of the
> major themes of this pamphlet, that "the law" is rarely as clear as proponents
> of one side of an argument suggest that it is. Most of the examples used in
> the pamphlet involve aspects of the law that supporters of the CAM believe
> to be clear, and clearly violated by United States policies; the *Curtiss-Wright*
> example shows that "the law" doesn't clearly support United States policy
> either.

approval resolutions would not be submitted to the President, on the
theory that the initial delegation enhanced the President's power a lot
while the legislative veto reduced it only a little.

The Supreme Court's legislative veto case, *Immigration and
Naturalization Service v. Chadha,* shows, albeit in a particularly unat-
tractive setting, how the legislative veto works.[4] The immigration laws
say that people who overstay their visas can be deported. They also
allow the Attorney General to suspend the deportation if deportation
would lead to extreme hardship. Congress gave the Attorney General
the power to suspend deportation so that it would no longer have to
consider passing private bills allowing named individuals to remain in
the United States. But, in exchange for giving the Attorney General the
power to suspend deportation, Congress required reports on suspensions and created a legislative veto: if either house voted to disapprove
a suspension, the person would be deported. In 1975 the Attorney
General sent Congress a list of 340 suspensions. A House subcommittee reviewed the list and decided that six of the people, including Chadha, would not suffer "extreme hardship" if they were deported. It
recommended that the legislative veto be exercised, and it was.

The Supreme Court held that all legislative vetoes are unconstitutional. Chadha was not deported, and probably shouldn't have been:
the chair of the subcommittee had misrepresented to the House what
the consequences of the veto would be. But the Court's decision went
well beyond Chadha's situation. It said that legislative vetoes were unconstitutional because they effectively repealed laws without the President having a say in the matter. According to the Court, the Constitution
required that laws be passed by both houses of Congress and signed
(or vetoed) by the President.

The Chadha decision has been almost universally criticized by
scholars on the ground that it invokes an extremely rigid idea of separation of powers to prohibit a useful mechanism for balancing presidential and congressional power. For example, Congress tried to use
legislative vetoes to control arms sales, allowing certain sales to take
place only if Congress did not disapprove—veto—within thirty days of

being notified about the proposed sales. This let Congress bargain with the President over what exactly could be sold. Take away the legislative veto, and what can Congress do? It could try to enact legislation blocking specific sales, but the President can veto such proposals, and the President's veto can be overridden only by a two-thirds vote in both houses, rather than by a majority vote in one. Congress can also try to limit the President politically. Sometimes, Congress has required the President to report on his plans, and wait for thirty days before carrying them out. Sometimes, Congress has allowed the President to spend money only if he makes a specific finding; for example, United States aid to the government of El Salvador can be sent only if the President finds that the human rights situation there is improving. Obviously these "findings" requirements don't mean much legally. They can help the political position of people who oppose the President. Findings can be attacked as ridiculous. Opponents can use the time between reporting plans and carrying them out to make it harder politically to carry out the plans than it would be if the President could act first and report later. All this is harder without the legislative veto than it was with it.

As we'll see, it's important not to overestimate the actual impact of the Chadha decision. For now, what's important is the fact that the Supreme Court endorsed the President's position in a dispute with Congress. The relative power of the President should be increased, according to the Court.

The Supreme Court has shown its sympathy for enhanced presidential power in other separation of powers cases as well. Two cases involving the effects of foreign policy on important domestic interests are particularly illuminating.

The Iranian Hostage case—One central issue in the Iranian hostage case was whether the Constitution allowed the President to prevent United States companies from pursuing their legal claims against Iran.[5] As part of the arrangements for Iran's release of hostages, President Carter agreed to set up a special international court to decide all claims against Iran, such as claims that Iran had breached its commercial contracts. Some United States corporations had already filed suit in United States courts, and the agreement required President Carter to suspend such suits. Although several statutes deal with methods of settling international commercial claims, none of them specifically authorized the President to suspend pending lawsuits. The constitutional problem was that the President seemed to be acting "lawlessly," that is, without any law saying that he could suspend claims. Relying on "the general tenor of Congress' legislation," the Supreme Court upheld the President's action. In the area of foreign policy, it said, Congress did not have to spell out what the President could do. The President's power to initiate action, even without specific congressional authority, was affirmed.

Travel to Cuba—The Court also strained to uphold presidential action in a case restricting travel to Cuba.[6] Before 1977, Congress had given the President broad authority to restrict trade in peacetime "emergencies." Concerned that Presidents had abused this power by inventing emergencies, Congress in 1977 attempted to limit the power to declare a national emergency. The statute had a "grandfather" provision that allowed the President to continue to exercise authority as to "emergencies" that had been declared before 1977. President Kennedy had declared an emergency with respect to Cuba in 1962, and had restricted some aspects of trade with Cuba. Twenty years later, the Reagan administration substantially expanded those restrictions. The Court held (5-4) that the grandfather provision allowed the President to do whatever he chose, rather than limiting him to enforcing only those restrictions actually in place in 1977. To do that, the Court had to read the statutes selectively and distort a legislative history that showed fairly clearly that Congress simply wanted to keep the 1977 restrictions in effect.

Other cases could be added to this list,[7] but the pattern is clear: as between the President and Congress, the Supreme Court prefers the President. The consequences are reasonably clear too. In recent years Congress has been more sensitive than the President to concerns about the domestic impact of foreign policy. It's possible that Congress would have adopted the Reagan administration's restrictions on travel to Cuba, but it would not have been as easy as doing it by presidential decree. When the Supreme Court systematically backs the President in cases like these, it makes it easier for the United States government to pursue an aggressive and interventionist foreign policy.

That's not to say that Supreme Court decisions restricting the President's power would dramatically reverse the course of foreign policy. The disagreements between the President and Congress take place within a framework of substantial agreement among political elites about the proper role of the United States in world affairs—the sustained consensus that plays a central part in the theory of the Constitution.

The effects of this consensus are illustrated rather well by what has happened to the War Powers Resolution, which was Congress's attempt to put some limits on the President's ability to send United States

TABLE THREE

The War Powers Resolution in Practice

Evacuation of United States citizens from Cyprus, 1974
No prior consultation, no report filed

Evacuations from Indochina, 1975
Prior information about intentions, report filed immediately follow-ing action evacuating DaNang, stating, "In accordance with my desire to keep the Congress fully informed on this matter, and taking note of the provisions" of the War Powers Resolution; no consultation prior to evacua-tion of Phnom Penh, during congressional recess, report filed on day fol-lowing evacuation, in same terms as DaNang report; third report filed after evacuation of Saigon, "taking note" of War Powers Resolution

The *Mayaguez* affair, May 12-15, 1975
Ten House and eleven Senate leaders informed that President Ford would probably use some sort of force, on evening before major force used (though armed forces "introduced" into area earlier); report filed within forty-eight hours (at 2:30 A.M.)

Evacuation of United States citizens from Lebanon, June 18, 1976
No consultation because efforts to reach members of Congress after adjournment for day failed; two reports filed

Iran Rescue attempt, 1980
No consultation prior to termination of effort; report filed "because of my desire that Congress be informed on this matter and consistent with the reporting provisions of the War Powers Resolution"

Lebanon, 1982
(See discussion in text)

Invasion of Grenada, October 1983
No prior consultation, though congressional leaders notified of im-pending invasion on the night before it occurred; report filed "consistent with the War Powers Resolution"

military forces into combat situations. (Although it is technically called a "Resolution," it has the same effect as a statute because it passed both the House and the Senate, was submitted to and vetoed by President Nixon in 1973, and then adopted when the veto was overridden.) The War Powers Resolution requires the President to consult with Congress "in *every possible instance*" before sending military forces into hos-tilities, and to report to Congress within forty-eight hours after sending them, explaining why they were sent and how long they are expected to remain. The Resolution also requires that troops be withdrawn after ninety days, or earlier if Congress passes a concurrent resolution (which can't be vetoed by the President). Since its enactment, Presidents have ignored the War Powers Resolution. When Grenada was invaded, President Reagan "consulted" Congress by informing some leaders that the invasion would occur a few hours later. Presidents have submitted reports, about the Iranian hostage rescue attempt and the bombing of Cambodia in connection with the effort to recapture the merchant ship *Mayaguez*, but they have always said that they were reporting not to comply with the War Powers Resolution but rather out of courtesy to Congress. (See Table Three.) Nothing significant has ever happened to damage a President, politically or legally, for ignoring the War Powers Resolution. The reasons should be clear by now: United States military action has taken place within a framework of broad agreement among the governing elites about what United States interests are and almost as broad agreement about how they are to be advanced. Once the President takes the initiative, that consensus makes it difficult for members of Congress to oppose his actions on what at that point seem to be mere matters of detail.

The interaction between President and Congress in 1983 over the presence of United States troops in Lebanon dramatically illustrates the operative meaning of the constitutional separation of powers. Troops were sent to Lebanon in 1982 as a "peacekeeping" force. Because President Reagan did not regard the situation as involving the use of United States troops in "hostilities," he didn't attempt to comply with the War Powers Resolution. By the fall of 1983, the troops were engaged in substantial defensive activities, and in September a United States warship shelled targets in Lebanon. At that point it was clear that the troops had become involved in hostilities. The ninety-day limit in the War Powers Resolution should have been triggered. But it wasn't. Instead, Congress "compromised," enacting a joint resolution (which President Reagan signed) allowing the troops to stay in Lebanon for up to eighteen months, far longer than Reagan wanted them there anyway.

The Lebanon episode is an almost perfect expression of what the separation of powers means in foreign affairs today. The President and Congress must indeed bargain, as the framers expected. But the bargaining takes place within sharply defined bounds because policymakers in both branches agree on so much. And the President's ability to initiate action structures the bargaining process so that it tends to result in outcomes closer to what he wants, within those bounds, than to what Congress wants.

CHAPTER THREE

Civil Liberties and National Security

When governing elites are not substantially divided, it's difficult to use the courts to advance a political goal at odds with the policies of the President and Congress. At those times, the courts usually act in accord with the other branches of government. As we have seen, that's true for most of what the courts do. But it is particularly true where the government violates civil liberties in the name of national security.

A good way to see this is by examining a series of cases involving illegal surveillance, violations of free speech, and restrictions on the free exercise of religion. And a good way to begin is with a recent case that is more important for its expression of the Court's views on national security than for its result. *Goldman v. Weinberger* involved an Orthodox Jew in the Air Force who was disciplined for wearing a yarmulke.[1] That violated an Air Force regulation prohibiting nonregulation headgear. (Goldman had worn his yarmulke for several years without attracting attention, but got into trouble after he testified as a defense witness at a court-martial.) Goldman claimed that applying the regulation to him violated his constitutional right to free exercise of religion. He relied on cases that found such violations in denying unemployment benefits to Seventh Day Adventists who lost their jobs because they couldn't work on Saturdays. Goldman argued that these cases showed that governments had to "accommodate" religious belief in their rules.

The Supreme Court, in a 5-4 decision, rejected Goldman's claim. It did not say that it would be hard for the Air Force to accommodate Goldman's religious rights. Instead, it said that it was "far more deferential" to military regulations than to civilian ones like the unemployment

Box Six

THE LAW AND THE CAM

One way to divide the ways in which the CAM is involved with the law is to distinguish between civil law and criminal law. Civil law involves efforts to obtain money from people who have harmed you, or to prevent the government from continuing to conduct illegal operations, by getting the courts to issue an injunction against those operations. Creative crafting of a case, combined with public education and outreach, can be of great benefit to the CAM.

The CAM can be involved in civil cases as plaintiffs or as defendants. As plaintiffs some elements of the CAM have sued to recover damages resulting from the attempt on the life of Eden Pastora. In that suit the plaintiffs are able to invoke the power of the federal court to compel discovery, that is, to force the defendants—including government officials—to reveal information in their hands about their own operations. (But there are important limitations on what plaintiffs will be allowed to discover in that way.) CAM plaintiffs might also sue the government for damages resulting from harassment of the CAM, or they might try to enjoin harassment. (Some limitations on the ability to obtain such an injunction are discussed in the text in connection with *Laird v. Tatum*.)

The CAM can be defendants in civil cases when the government seeks to deport refugees from Central America, discriminating against refugees from El Salvador and in favor of those from Nicaragua on political grounds. A refugee from El Salvador, who is a defendant in a deportation proceeding, can raise the political discrimination issue by arguing that such discrimination is inconsistent with the requirements of the deportation statute.

Criminal cases involving the CAM include prosecutions in Sanctuary cases for conspiracy to violate the immigration laws, and ordinary trespass cases against CAM activists who try to obstruct recruiting on college campuses by the Central Intelligence Agency. Obviously the CAM cannot control when criminal cases are brought, as they can when they are plaintiffs in civil cases. But the CAM's concerns for criminal violations of the law in connection with the Iran-contra affair, as well as violations of the Neutrality Act in private support for the contras, show that the CAM can attempt to build public support for certain kinds of criminal prosecutions.

statutes. The Court said that it had to "give great deference to the professional judgment of military authorities," who had made a "reasonable" judgment that standardized uniforms "encourage the subordination of personal preferences and identities in favor of the overall group mission." Even though the Air Force allows people to wear personalized rings and bracelets, and it would be easy to exempt people with religious objections from the headgear regulations, the Air Force didn't have to do anything to accommodate Goldman's beliefs.

We will return to the free exercise problem later. For now, *Goldman* is important because it illustrates the Court's willingness to tolerate restrictions on civil liberties, for no especially good reason, when the government says that national security interests are at stake. This same abdication is apparent in other civil liberties cases involving (1) free speech, (2) political surveillance, and (3) religious liberty.

1. Free Speech and "Border Control": The CAM is particularly interested in presenting voters in the United States with perspectives on Central America that differ from the official ones. Frequently the best sources of this information are Central Americans. The immigration laws authorize the government to restrict entry into the United States even by temporary visitors. Until recently one provision barred entry to noncitizens who belong to organizations that promote communism, but directed that this prohibition should be waived except in national security cases. Another provision prohibited entry to those whose activities in the United States "would be prejudicial to the public interest." The Reagan administration interpreted this to allow it to bar entry to people whose speeches to United States audiences would criticize United States foreign policy. Among those excluded on the ground that their admission would be "prejudicial to the public interest" have been Gabriel Garcia Marquez, Carlos Fuentes, and Julio Cortazar, all prominent writers among whose positions has been opposition to United States policy in Central America.[2] Legal and political challenges to these actions led Congress in 1987 to repeal the provisions authorizing them.

The Supreme Court held a century ago that the people seeking entry didn't have any rights under the Constitution, but what about the people in the United States who want to hear what the visitors have to say? In 1972 the Court agreed that the first amendment's protection of free speech did give the audience a right to receive information, but held that the restrictions on entry didn't violate that right.[3] It upheld the denial of a visa to the Belgian Marxist Ernest Mandel, who had planned a speaking tour, and said that the rights of audiences in the United States weren't violated so long as the government offered a "facially valid" national security justification for the exclusion. That is, the government merely has to tell the court that it has a reason which, if it were supported by facts, would justify the exclusion, but it doesn't have to provide the court with any factual support for its claim.

We've seen that the government can also make it difficult for people from the United States to travel to places that the government doesn't want them to see. It can take away their passports and bar them from spending money in those countries. It probably can't make it a crime simply to travel to those countries, and in fact the government has not done much to impede travel to Central America (aside from Cuba). The Court has made it clear, though, that travel restrictions would not violate the Constitution.

2. Political Surveillance: Civil liberties are also invaded when the government engages in surveillance of political activities. Surveillance can include break-ins that disrupt an organization's activities, or wiretaps and covert monitoring that may scare people away from the movement. Political surveillance might violate the free speech guarantees of the first amendment, or the protection against unreasonable searches and seizures contained in the fourth amendment. Once again, the Court has made it clear that the Constitution provides little protection where surveillance is based on asserted national security concerns.

a. Free Speech: The Court used one of the avoidance devices discussed in Chapter One to dismiss a free speech challenge to political surveillance. *Laird v. Tatum* involved protestors against the Vietnam War who challenged surveillance by the Army.[4] The protestors argued that surveillance deterred people from joining the movement. The 5-4 decision by the Court held that the claim was "unripe." It said that, to get the courts to rule on the constitutional issue, the protestors would have to show that someone actually had been deterred or that the Army had misused the information it gathered to harm the protestors. Of course, it is almost impossible to find someone who will say that she stayed away from political protests only because she was afraid of Army surveillance; after all, by saying that, she would be identifying herself as exactly the kind of person the Army wanted to keep tabs on. And the secrecy of the surveillance made it equally difficult to discover "abuses" of the information the Army gathered.

(Another aspect of *Laird v. Tatum* drives home the theme that judges are political actors. When he was in the Department of Justice, William Rehnquist testified at a congressional hearing that he believed that Army surveillance of political protest was constitutional. Even though he had expressed his view on both the issue and the Laird case itself, Rehnquist was one of the five Justices who voted to reject the protestors' challenge. If he had not participated in the Supreme Court decision, the Court would have been divided equally, which would have let the case proceed so that the protestors might have found out about the "abuses" the Court said they had to know about beforehand.)

b. Illegal Searches: The fourth amendment requires that, in general, judges issue warrants before government agents can conduct a search or place a wiretap. The Court held that warrants *were* required for surveillance of a purely domestic political group.[5] It carefully limited its discussion to domestic groups, and its care has been taken to mean that surveillance of groups that are "connected to" foreign countries can be conducted without getting a warrant. In 1978 Congress passed the Foreign Intelligence Surveillance Act, which sets up a procedure for getting warrants for wiretaps on "agents" of foreign countries. The Act does say that no United States "person"—citizen or lawfully admitted alien—can be placed under surveillance solely because of activities protected by the first amendment.

These kinds of guarantees are almost toothless. In most situations, government officials will be protected from going to jail or paying damages to victims of illegal surveillance if the officials reasonably believed that the surveillance was legal. The Court's hints about national security wiretapping, and the likelihood that an official could point to something other than first amendment activities as the basis for surveillance, would make it easy for officials to show that they reasonably believed that what they were doing was all right. No application for a wiretap under the 1978 Act has ever been denied.[6] Surveillance is almost by definition clandestine. The targets may suspect that they are being watched, but they will rarely be able to prove it on their own. In the past, disclosures about illegal surveillance have been made in connection with more general investigations, which themselves demonstrate substantial division among ruling elites. When that sort of division occurs, the courts may be willing to find that another part of the government acted illegally. Under such circumstances, the targets of political surveillance may be able to exploit these divisions and establish the illegality of what happened, perhaps even strengthening opposition to the policies. Otherwise, it's unlikely that challenges to surveillance will get very far.

3. Religious Liberty: Finally, we can consider the free exercise of religion problem. Within the CAM, the Sanctuary effort attempts to provide refuge for Central Americans driven from their homes because of United States policy, in the face of United States programs aimed at keeping these Central Americans out of the country. Some Sanctuary activists have been convicted of violating United States immigration laws. So far the courts have rejected the legal defenses offered by

Sanctuary defendants. In particular, the courts have not agreed that convictions should be prohibited because the Sanctuary activists were following the commands of their religions in assisting the Central American refugees. (See Box Seven.)

The result in the Goldman case, where much less—in terms of United States policy—was at stake, should make this result no surprise. The courts have had trouble figuring out how to deal with free exercise claims. As in the Sanctuary cases, these claims arise when the government has a regulation—the headgear rule in *Goldman,* the immigration laws in Sanctuary cases—that applies to everybody, but affects people with specific religious beliefs more severely than it affects others. The Supreme Court has said that, in such situations, the government must adjust its general rules to reduce the impact on religious believers, if it can do so without substantially undermining the goals its rules are trying to advance. The courts believe that enforcing restrictions on immigration is a major goal of United States domestic and foreign policy, and they therefore are unlikely to require that the immigration laws make any accommodation to religious belief.

When we look at all of these areas as a group, the pattern is obvious. No matter what the precise legal test is in any area, once the government invokes national security to justify its actions, the courts will probably go along. The general structure of the government, in light of the degree of consensus among political elites about what national security means, makes that what we should expect.

4. Demonstrations: Demonstrations also raise civil liberties issues, and here the picture is a little more encouraging. Since the 1960s the law has been clear that the government must permit ordinary demonstrations—those in which people assemble, march through the streets, and listen to speeches. Such demonstrations play an important part in building a movement. They allow people who are slightly committed to the movement to deepen their commitment by seeing that there are lots of other people who agree with them. Demonstrations can also build solidarity among elements of a diverse movement. To some extent, the publicity associated with ordinary demonstrations can attract additional supporters to the movement.

Yet, to the extent that publicity is important, an opposition movement like the CAM may run into civil liberties obstacles. The first amendment requires that the government allow *ordinary* demonstrations. But, except in special circumstances, ordinary demonstrations may not generate the publicity the movement might want. If it is concerned with publicity, the movement may have to develop innovative types of

Box Seven

THE SANCTUARY TRIAL IN ARIZONA

On January 14, 1985, sixteen Sanctuary workers were indicted for violating federal laws restricting immigration into the United States. The indictment was based in large part on information provided by a government agent who had infiltrated church activities, including planning of Sanctuary efforts. Charges were later dropped against five of the workers. The remaining defendants—including two Roman Catholic priests, a nun, a Presbyterian minister, and other church workers—were tried in October 1985 before federal judge Earl Carroll, a conservative Carter appointee who had represented large Arizona mining companies before he became a judge.

Judge Carroll was hostile to the defendants from the outset. He rejected the defendats' legal arguments that international law required them to aid the refugees they helped, and barred them from presenting evidence about conditions in Central America. After the government put on what many observers thought was a fairly weak case, the defendants did not call any witnesses on their behalf—in part because of the apparent weakness of the case against them, and in part because Judge Carroll's rulings made it impossible for them to present to the jury the kind of evidence that the defendants thought was most important.

Judge Carroll instructed the jury to consider only whether the defendants had done acts that amounted to violations of the immigration laws. The defendants did not deny that they had committed most of those acts, but wanted to show that their actions were justified by international law and religious motives. But the judge did not instruct the jury to consider such matters. And, in line with standard practice, the jury was not informed of its power to acquit defendants even if law violations, in a strict sense, had occurred.

Eight of the eleven defendants were convicted. Interviewed after the trial, several jurors said that they "felt really bad" about the convictions, but believed that they had to follow the law and convict the defendants. After delivering a lecture to the defendants on working within the system, Judge Carroll gave them probation and suspended sentences.

demonstrations—shantytowns to protest apartheid, obstruction of CIA recruiting, and the like. A series of decisions by the Supreme Court has made it reasonably clear that the government does not have to allow innovative demonstrations. For example, people seeking more government aid for the homeless were allowed to erect symbolic tent cities near the White House, but the government would not let them sleep overnight in the tents. The Supreme Court upheld this ban on "camping" as a reasonable regulation that allowed the parks to be kept "at-tractive" and that was not aimed specifically at any particular point of view—even though no one other than the homeless and their supporters had a viewpoint that would be expressed by sleeping in a tent.[7]

The civil liberties picture for the CAM is not entirely grim. Ordinary demonstrations have to be allowed. Also, the government must have the political will to enforce its rules against the CAM. Sometimes enforcing the rules can be quite costly. Jailing "respectable" religious people can discredit the government's enforcement policies and build support for the CAM. And, as we have seen, once an opposition movement becomes strong enough, the courts may sometimes side with it against the executive branch.

The surveillance problem exposes a more important dimension of the civil liberties issue. We have seen that it's unlikely that the courts would find that illegal surveillance had occurred, or would penalize any official for ordering illegal surveillance. But it's also pretty clear that such officials would be damaged politically if word of their conduct got out. It wouldn't matter much that the courts refused to find that their activities were illegal. Indeed, in some circumstances the CAM may not be harmed, and may even be assisted by decisions that openly reject the movement's civil liberties claims. That occurs because the law, in addition to being a means of maintaining the system and a vehicle for expressing disagreements within the governing coalition, is also an expression of some of our society's highest aspirations. This aspirational role of the law comes into focus in the chapter that follows.

CHAPTER FOUR

Social Movements and the Aspirations of Law

So far we have examined how the courts enforce the law. In general they enforce it to sustain an existing consensus among political elites, but sometimes opposition political movements can take advantage of divisions among those elites to use the law to advance their political goals. This focus on courts is not unusual in discussions about law. After all, most of the time we think about law so that we can figure out what will happen to us if we do something. (See Box One on the "bad man" theory of law.) And judges along with other officials are the people who will enforce the law.

But there's another perspective we could take. Law can be seen as something more than, or different from, what public officials do. The last chapter ended by introducing the idea that, to some extent, the law can be seen as expressing popular aspirations for justice. Opposition political movements in the United States have nurtured a tradition of appeals to what some have called the higher law of the Constitution. Of course people often appeal to a higher law in politics; there are purely moral arguments, for example that United States policy in Central America is immoral even if it is entirely legal. But the appeal to the higher law of the Constitution is different. That appeal sometimes works because the Constitution embodies important aspirations to justice that many people share. Those aspirations, rather than the official interpretations of the Constitution, are "the Constitution," according to the higher law view.

In that view the United States is a democratic republic dedicated to the pursuit of justice according to law. Its officials often fall short of accomplishing those aspirations, and even deny the relevance of justice when they insist that the United States must pursue a "realistic" foreign policy in which concern for justice is subordinated to concern for the defense of a narrowly defined national interest. But, according to this view, the people of the United States believe that their country embodies fundamental ideals of humanity. When officials deviate from those ideals, they are violating the law no matter how many judges say that the officials' actions are lawful.

International law is, in some of its aspects, an expression of these aspirations to justice in international relations. It is striking that the United States government was so fearful of the application of international law to its activities in Nicaragua that it attempted to withdraw from proceedings before the World Court in which it would have been forced to justify those activities. The World Court refused to accept the United States' withdrawal and found that the activities—which included the mining of Nicaraguan harbors and some forms of support for the contras—did violate international law. In doing so the World Court expressed the aspirations of law towards justice.

Those aspirations have implications for political strategy using law in the United States as well. A brief review of the structure of international law, and of some of the CAM's arguments that United States policy violates international law, will show how.

International law has two components: treaties that the United States has signed, and customary law, which is defined by finding out what are nearly universal practices by the world's nations. The Constitution says that, like the Constitution itself, treaties made by the United States are "the supreme law of the land," and courts have held that customary international law binds the United States as well.[1] What that means is unclear.

Like all legal documents—including, as we have seen, the Constitution—most treaties are ambiguous. In addition, it's often nearly impossible to define exactly what customary international law prohibits. The practices of the world's nations vary a lot, and it's usually pretty easy to explain a departure from widespread practices by pointing to some special characteristics of the situation at hand that aren't present in the ordinary case. For example, the United States government frequently claims that its special responsibilities as a superpower allow it to do things—including intervene in other countries' affairs—that are prohibited to other nations. Because customary international law is defined by actual practices, and because superpower interventions are in fact frequent, it's hard to evaluate that claim in any definitive way. Finally, international law lacks any authoritative interpreters. The courts in the United States interpret the Constitution, and can order people to comply with it. The World Court, in contrast, has no power to compel governments to follow its orders. All it can do is say what it believes international law is. Governments that want to go along—or are compelled to by political pressure—will do so. But they don't have to.

What are the CAM's international law arguments against United States policy? Again, it's important to stress at the outset that, in light of the uncertain status of international law, the point of these arguments is to appeal to widely-shared notions of justice.

Most modern treaties fit into the framework established by the Charter of the United Nations, which prohibits "the threat or use of force against the territorial integrity or political independence of any state." The Charter of the Organization of American States denies any government "the right to intervene, directly or indirectly, for any reason whatever, in the internal or external affairs of any State." It prohibits "the use of coercive measures of an economic or political character in order to force the sovereign will of another State." Customary international law is less well-defined, but it prohibits aggressive war and limits the techniques that can be used in conducting war, as the World Court held in the Nicaragua case. Virtually the only limit to the ban on the use of force is self-defense. The UN Charter allows self-defense against an armed attack, until the UN itself takes steps to maintain or restore peace. In international law, self-defense must be limited; it cannot involve reprisals or counter-aggression, and can be directed only at immediate threats to a nation.

The case that United States activities in Central America violate international law is overwhelming. The declared policy of the United States is the replacement of the government of Nicaragua, by means of support for the contras. No more direct intervention into a state's internal affairs can be imagined. Nor is it plausible to contend that supporting the contras is necessary for the "self-defense" of the United States or the nations it supports in the region.

Defenders of United States government policy usually do not even try to argue that the policy is consistent with international law. Instead, they insist that people should treat international law as a grab-bag of vague rhetoric, to be used only when it helps advance the interests of the United States in its various superpower enterprises.[2] International law, to them, is just politics.

In one sense, that's right. International law doesn't have any of the enforcement mechanisms that we usually associate with "real" law. No one can invoke international law to force an unwilling United States or Soviet Union to change its policies. The World Court issues advisory opinions; the courts of the United States will enforce international law against the President or Congress only if the courts are backed up by a powerful popular movement that wants international law enforced.

But international law can play a role in international and domestic politics because it is, in part, aspirational. The very discomfort that intervention's defenders express by deprecating international law is suggestive. After all, they don't say that the United States Constitution is "just politics." They have to minimize the importance of international law because they understand that it isn't as vague as they would like, and because they are at a political disadvantage when the CAM invokes international law against them.

What's at stake is, Who decides what the law "is"? Defenders of United States government policy tend to adopt the "bad man" theory of law, at least to the extent of saying that the law "is" what officials in the United States who have power to enforce their views, say it is. The alternative is that the people decide what the law is.

The tradition that there is a higher law of the Constitution embodies this alternative. A useful example comes from the movement to abolish slavery before the Civil War. Some abolitionists developed an interpretation of the Constitution according to which slavery was unconstitutional because it deprived slaves of life, liberty, and property without due process of law. Every official interpreter of the Constitution—courts, Congress, the President—rejected that theory. To the abolitionists, that rejection was irrelevant. The Constitution meant what it meant, no matter what the courts or other official interpreters said.

This higher law tradition remains important. But it's crucial to understand that this tradition involves the people in deciding what the law is. Attorney General Meese offered a bastardized version of the tradition in his argument that the decisions of the Supreme Court were not the supreme law of the land, and that officials like him could lawfully disregard Supreme Court decisions. But the higher law tradition is not really about how officials should behave. It's about what responsible people in the United States ought to do when they see the United States government doing things that, as they analyze the law, are illegal. One thing they can do is appeal to the higher law tradition, forcefully presenting their legal arguments not simply to the courts, which may reject them, but to the public.

Important prospects for political strategies using law open up once we see law as an appeal to widely shared aspirations. The aim of such strategies is to make the United States government more and more

Box Eight

The Pros and Cons of Litigation

It is expensive to be involved in a lawsuit. For plaintiffs, the costs of engaging in discovery can be quite substantial. It's easy to start a lawsuit; you simply have to develop some facts and then file a complaint in the court. But it can be expensive to pursue a case once it has been filed. Particularly in highly political cases like those that the CAM might bring, government and private defendants are likely to do everything they can to delay the case. CAM plaintiffs and their lawyers may spend lots of time trying to push the case along. For defendants, especially in criminal cases, the stakes are so high that people will spend a lot of time and money in trying to avoid imprisonment.

In any effort, activists have to spend time raising money to support their work. In legal matters costs are generally high, and when activists are involved in litigation much of the money they raise will have to be used for the lawsuit rather than other political activities. On the other hand, some people will contribute money to a legal defense fund who would not contribute to an overtly political effort. Thus legal work can sometimes support important political organizing efforts. Moreover, legal work brings certain legitimacy and credibility with it that other efforts sometimes lack, and can therefore claim the attention of entirely new groups of citizens.

In addition, people who get involved in lawsuits can become emotionally involved in winning the lawsuit, and overlook the broader political setting. When you're a defendant in a criminal case, that's completely understandable. But unless the case is part of a broader political strategy, with substantial resources allocated to organizing, it can reduce the amount of effort spent on general political work.

distant from increasing numbers of people who share the aspirations that government policy rejects. The strategies can take many forms. For example, the World Court's decision, though ignored by the Reagan administration, has demonstrated that government policy violates international law. The World Court's judgment has influenced debates in Congress and public opinion in the United States and throughout the world. Similarly, criminal prosecutions in Sanctuary cases sometimes can provide opportunities for publicity about why people flee Central America. Civil suits can seek to expose government illegality. Prosecutions for demonstrating against the CIA can be met by the defense that interfering with the CIA is necessary in order to prevent greater violations of law by the CIA itself. And whatever happens in court, lawsuits, including the defense of criminal prosecutions, provide important opportunities for political education. It's not difficult to shift the focus of attention outside the courtroom from what the defendants did to what the government did.

Of course there are also important limitations on the use of such political-legal strategies. (See Box Eight.) Even so, real opportunities do exist. One reason returns us to some of the considerations about the general structure of government with which this pamphlet began. Federalism means, among other things, that it is possible for opposition movements like the CAM to obtain significant toeholds in particular cities and states well before it is able to influence policymakers in Washington to the same extent. Careful organization on the local level can produce victories in court, such as the acquittals obtained in Northampton, Massachusetts of activists who interfered with CIA recruiting. And policymakers in Washington may find it difficult to ignore the signals that those sorts of victories send about public views on the policy of the government.

CHAPTER FIVE

Conclusion

We began this pamphlet by contrasting the CAM's powerful arguments against the legality of United States policy in Central America with some skeptical observations about how unlikely it was that anything would come of those arguments in the courts—the usual forums for legal arguments. If anything, the rest of the pamphlet should have increased our skepticism about *that*.

But it should also have explained why the CAM's legal arguments are important in building opposition to United States policy in Central America—because they represent one way to express the aspirations of many people in the United States to live in a country seeking peace and justice.

The CAM's international law arguments show that the courts are not the only forums for legal arguments. The appeal to the higher law of the Constitution shows the same thing. These arguments are made in the political arena too, where they express aspirations that the CAM believes to be widely shared and knows to be violated by United States policy. They work in the political arena because law—international, constitutional, and statutory—is more than what courts say it is. Law does a lot of things. Of course it supports the existing social order, which is why we should be skeptical about using law to undermine that order. But law also expresses widely held aspirations about what kind of society we ought to have. By doing that, the law does more than support a social order. It also helps shape, and provides the opportunity to reshape, our society.

It's not simply that we would like the law to express these aspirations. It already does. When the CAM argues that United States policy is illegal, then, it means that the policy is inconsistent with aspirations embodied in the law *as it is now*.

Sometimes courts will respond by enforcing those aspirations. But even if they don't, public discussion of United States policy can be shaped by invoking the law as one of many expressions of our aspirations.

NOTES

Introduction

1. *Nicaragua v. United States*, 1986 I.C.J. 14. (Citations to court decisions usually begin with the volume number, followed by the official name of the reporting system on the first page of the court's opinion. Thus, *Nicaragua v. United States* begins on p. 14 of the volume designated 1986 in the reports of the International Court of Justice.)

2. Intelligence Authorization Act for FY 1985, Pub. L. No. 98-618, sec. 801.

3. See Report of the President's Special Review Board (*The Tower Commission Report*), Appendix C.

4. 18 U.S.C. sec. 960. (This is a provision in Title 18, the criminal code, of the United States Code of laws.)

5. See *Tower Commission Report*, Appendix C.

6. The district court's decision dismissing the lawsuit is unreported. At this writing the case is pending on appeal.

7. See *Dellums v. Smith*, 797 F.2d 817 (9th Cir. 1986).

8. These arguments were rejected in *Nicaragua v. United States*, 1984 I.C.J. 392.

9. The activities of the United States government in Central America are extensive, are illegal in many ways, and are revealed only piecemeal. Any effort to describe in detail particular illegalities would become rapidly outdated. The best sources of information on the legal aspects of United States activities in Central America are the National Lawyers Guild, 853 Broadway, Suite 1705, New York, NY 10003, and the Center for Constitutional Rights, 853 Broadway, Suite 1401, New York, NY 10003. A partial overview, identifying the legal issues raised by the Iran-contra affair but not drawing legal conclusions, is David Scheffer, "U.S. Law and the Iran-Contra Affair," 81 *American Journal of International Law* 696 (1987).

Chapter One

1. For general discussions of the period, see John Fiske, *The Critical Period of American History, 1783-1789* (1888), and Merrill Jensen, *The Articles of Confederation* (1963).

2. See Morton Horwitz, *The Transformation of American Law, 1780-1860* (1977).

3. Federalist 51.

4. Michael Parenti, *The Anti-Communist Impulse* (1969).

5. The following account is based on E.P. Thompson, *Whigs and Hunters: The Origins of the Black Act* (1975), and Michael Tigar & Madeleine Levy, *Law and the Rise of Capitalism* (1977).

6. *Lochner v. New York*, 198 U.S. 45 (1905) (invalidating statute setting maximum hours for bakers); *Coppage v. Kansas*, 236 U.S. 1 (1915) (invalidating state law prohibiting employers from refusing to employ members of labor unions).

7. See, e.g., *Allied Structural Steel Co. v. Spannaus*, 438 U.S. 234 (1978); *Nollan v. California Coastal Commission*, 107 S.Ct. 3141 (1987).

8. This account is based on David Kairys, "Freedom of Speech," in David Kairys, ed., *The Politics of Law: A Progressive Critique* (1982).

9. Martin Shapiro, "Fathers and Sons: The Court, the Commentators, and the Search for Values," in Vincent Blasi, ed., *The Burger Court: The Counterrevolution That Wasn't* (1983).

10. *Brown v. Board of Education*, 354 U.S. 483 (1954).

11. The brief is reprinted in Tom Clark and Phillip Perlman, *Prejudice and Property* (1948).

12. *Valley Forge Christian College v. Americans United*, 454 U.S. 464 (1982).

13. *Baker v. Carr*, 369 U.S. 186 (1962).

14. See *Mora v. McNamara*, 389 U.S. 934 (1967) (Stewart, J., dissenting from denial of review).

15. *Goldwater v. Carter*, 444 U.S. 996 (1979). In this case Senator Barry Goldwater challenged the decision by President Carter to withdraw from a treaty of mutual defense with Taiwan, as part of the establishment of diplomatic relations with the Peoples Republic of China.

Chapter Two

1. The basic source on the issues discussed in this chapter is Louis Henkin, *Foreign Affairs and the Constitution* (1972).

2. *Forging Peace: The Challenge of Central America* (Basil Blackwell, 1987), by Richard Fagen offers an alternative policy for the region.

3. 299 U.S. 304 (1936).

4. 462 U.S. 919 (1983).

5. *Dames & Moore v. Regan*, 453 U.S. 654 (1981).

6. *Regan v. Wald*, 468 U.S. 222 (1984).

7. *Haig v. Agee*, 453 U.S. 280 (1981).

Chapter Three

1. 475 U.S. (1986).

2. Steven Shapiro, "Ideological Exclusions: Closing the Border to Political Dissidents," 100 *Harvard Law Review* 930 (1987).

3. *Kleindeinst v. Mandel*, 408 U.S. 753 (1972).

4. 408 U.S. 1 (1972).

5. *United States v. United States District Court (Keith)*, 407 U.S. 297 (1972).

6. See Helene Schwartz, "Oversight of Minimization Compliance under the Foreign Intelligence Surveillance Act: How the Watchdogs are Doing Their Jobs," 12 *Rutgers Law Journal* 405 (1981).

7. *Clark v. Community for Creative Non-Violence*, 468 U.S. 288 (1983).

Chapter Four

1. See Jules Lobel, "The Limits of Constitutional Power: Conflicts Between Foreign Policy and International Law," 71 *Virginia Law Review* 1071 (1985).

2. See, e.g., Charles Krauthammer, "Divided Superpower: The Real Cause of the North Affair," *New Republic*, 196 (Dec. 22, 1986): 14.

Mark Tushnet is a professor of Law at Georgetown University. He is the author of *Red, White, and Blue: Critical Analysis of Constitutional Law* and co-author of a casebook, *Constitutional Law*.

Professor Tushnet has written a thoughtful and insightful essay which explores both the usefulness and the limitations of law as a tool to halt U.S. military intervention in Central America.

—**Debra Evenson**
President, National Lawyers Guild

Can an illegal foreign policy be stopped in court? Mark Tushnet has done an invaluable service, by explaining what the Constitution and legal system mean for progressives trying to stop U.S. interventionism abroad.

—**Jules Lobel**
University of Pittsburgh Law School

This is an important and useful legal primer for Central America activists. It shatters the myths about the "neutrality" of U.S. law and situates legal questions where they really are: in the arena of political struggle. It shows how the law is used both by governing elites who share a consensus on keeping U.S. hegemony in Central America and by grassroots movements that push the limits of law and appeal to its underlying values to work for the self-determination of peoples in the region.

—**Maureen Fielder, S.L.**
Co-Director Quixote Center/Quest for Peace

A thoughtful analysis of the role of law in today's debate over U.S. policy in Central America.

—**Paul S. Reichler**
Counsel for Nicaragua in the World Court

This book should prove indispensable well beyond the Central America movement, an elegant short course on law and the legal system for activists everywhere. Definitely not Civics 101.

—**Duncan Kennedy**
Harvard Law School

SOUTH END PRESS   ISBN: 0-89608-340-3

$5.00   Political Science/Legal Studies/History

Cover graphic by John Klostner, design by Todd Jailer and Greg Bates